D1566059

South China Sea

Energy and Security Conflicts

Christopher L. Daniels

THE SCARECROW PRESS, INC.
Lanham • Toronto • Plymouth, UK
2014

Published by Scarecrow Press, Inc.
A wholly owned subsidiary of The Rowman & Littlefield Publishing Group, Inc.
4501 Forbes Boulevard, Suite 200, Lanham, Maryland 20706
http://www.scarecrowpress.com

Estover Road, Plymouth PL6 7PY, United Kingdom

British Library Cataloguing in Publication Information Available

Library of Congress Cataloging-in-Publication Data

Daniels, Christopher L., 1982- author.
South China Sea : energy and security conflicts / Christopher L. Daniels. pages cm. -- (Global flashpoints)
Includes bibliographical references and index.
ISBN 978-0-8108-8645-2 (cloth : alk. paper) -- ISBN 978-0-8108-8646-9 (ebook) 1. South China Sea region--Strategic aspects. 2. South China Sea--International status. 3. Security, International--South China Sea region. 4. Petroleum reserves--South China Sea region. 5. Natural gas reserves--South China Sea region. I. Title.
UA853.S68D36 2013
355'.033016472--dc23
2013019836

♾️ The paper used in this publication meets the minimum requirements of American National Standard for Information Sciences Permanence of Paper for Printed Library Materials, ANSI/NISO Z39.48-1992.

Printed in the United States of America

Contents

Acknowledgments

There are several people who were instrumental in the process of putting this book together. I first would like to thank Ms. Martha Freeman for her continued support throughout my career. Special gratitude is due to my research assistants: Sechaba Khoapa, Dionne Cargill, Mrs. Danielle Cross-Wilkins, Kyle Harris, and my personal editor, Ms. Esther Spencer. I also would like to thank my colleagues Dr. David Jackson, Dr. Gary Paul, Dr. Keith Simmonds, and Dr. Valencia Mathews for their assistance.

Gratitude is certainly owed to the whole staff over at Scarecrow Press for the work they have done with me over the years. Special acknowledgment is due to my series editor, Dr. Martin Gordon, and Bennett Graff, Andrew Yoder, Rayna Andrews, and everyone else whom I failed to mention by name.

Last, I would like to acknowledge my parents, Donald and Brenda Daniels; my brothers, Donald and Charleston; and my sister, Yolanda, for their continued love and support during this process.

ONE

Background and History of the South China Sea Dispute

The dispute over who will control the land and resources within the South China Sea (SCS) is quickly developing into one of the world's most significant geopolitical issues. Countries such as China, Vietnam, and Taiwan that have a claim to the territory also have rapidly growing economies that could be severely damaged if an armed conflict among them were to occur. Additionally, the world has developed a growing dependence on consumer goods manufactured in these Asian nations, and any significant reduction in the production of these products would have a dramatic effect on the global economy.

Despite the serious consequences a showdown could bring, the SCS and the origins of the dispute are still unknown to many, leaving a myriad of unanswered questions. This chapter addresses those questions by providing an in-depth examination of the history of the conflicting claims to the sea and the history of the naval and diplomatic disputes that have occurred as a result.[1]

DEFINING THE SOUTH CHINA SEA

The SCS stretches from Singapore and the Strait of Malacca in the southwest to the Strait of Taiwan in the northeast. The sea covers a radius of 1.4 million square miles and serves as a major transit point for Asian-manufactured goods. Nearly one third of the world's shipping transits through the sea, making the waterway crucial to the global economy. There are also hundreds of islands found in the region, most of which are uninhabited. The largest island chains are Spratly, Paracel, Pratas, and Scarborough Shoal. These islands themselves have very little economic value other than their strategic location, but this fact still has not prevented nearly every nation in the region from making conflicting claims to the territory. The main reason behind the intense claims to the sea is the belief that there could be billions, if not trillions, of dollars' worth of oil and natural gas found within the sea. Each respective nation needs these resources for continued industrial growth and to emerge or continue as dominant powers.[2]

CLAIMS TO THE SOUTH CHINA SEA

China, Taiwan, and Vietnam claim the SCS in its entirety. Malaysia, the Philippines, Indonesia, and Brunei, on the other hand, have only asserted ownerships over the islands that are close to their internationally recognized boundaries. Each country has developed its own basis for ownership in the areas that it has claimed, but the two most significant legal principles that apply here are the concepts of "effective occupation" and the United Nations Convention on the Law of the Sea (UNCLOS).[3]

The concept of effective occupation began to gain prominence as more and more territories that were formerly under some sort of colonial rule either began to gain independence or were transferred to other colonial powers. This reality created the need for an international legal framework to determine who had the right to claim ownership of a territory. One of the most famous legal cases dealing with this very issue was the case of the Island of Palmas.

Palmas is located in the Indian Ocean near Indonesia. In 1925, the United States and the Netherlands went in front of an international arbitration panel to determine who would gain ownership of the island. The United States claimed that it owned the territory because the Spanish had given the United States title to the Philippines after the 1898 Treaty of Paris. The Palmas Island was included within the boundaries of the land granted, so the United States assumed that it was also a part of the concession. In 1906, the United States discovered that the Netherlands also claimed the territory, and the two agreed to arbitration to determine the rightful owner.[4]

The judge ruled in favor of the Netherlands based on the concept of effective occupation. Even though the court did not dispute that Spain "discovered" the island first, it assessed that Spain did not take the necessary steps to govern the area. This lack of governance or control of the area, therefore, made Spain's and subsequently the United States' ownership claims invalid. This ruling set a precedent for the necessity of occupancy and control over an area to establish sovereignty. Several of the nations in the SCS region took notice of the ruling and adjusted their plans to assert ownership accordingly.[5]

The second legal framework that has shaped the SCS dispute is UN-CLOS. The treaty was the end result of a set of conferences spanning from 1973 to 1982. It took an additional twelve years for the agreement to gain the sixty signatures necessary for it to become effective. The law included some much-needed updates to the way maritime sovereignty was judged. For instance, in the past, three nautical miles from a nation's coastline was considered the end of its territorial waters. With the dramatic advances in technology during the nineteenth and twentieth centuries, nations required a much larger buffer zone to protect their interests.[6]

To adapt to these new needs, UNCLOS established different categories within the sea, each with a different set of rules. The first category is a nation's territorial waters, which extends twelve nautical miles from its coastline. In this area, the nation has absolute rights, but other nations still have the right to "innocent passage." However, even this right can be temporarily suspended or limited in certain instances. The second category is the contiguous zone, which extends out up to twenty-four nautical miles from the coast, and states have jurisdiction over this area. The final major category is the exclusive economic zone (EEZ), which extends up to two hundred nautical miles from a nation's shores. In this area, the respective nation has the exclusive right to any economically viable activities occurring in the waters. The two most common uses for the EEZ are to regulate deep-sea fishing and offshore oil exploration.[7]

With technology improving at such a rapid pace, nations are now able to benefit from resources that were previously undiscovered or thought to be unrecoverable. These adjustments in the law are steps in the right direction for the international community, but they also have made the disputes in the SCS a bit more complex. Because each of the nations are in close proximity to each other, it is almost inevitable that there would be conflicting claims. Some of the nations' claims are supported by recent international law, while others are viewed less favorably by those same laws.

CHINA

The nation whose claims have arguably suffered the most by the new interpretations of international law is China. China's case for ownership of the SCS is based on historical claims, which have very little weight in international law. As a result, China views current international law as a threat to its cultural heritage and has made efforts to circumvent it.

China argues that its claims predate UNCLOS and that the law should accommodate its historical rights. Its argument is based on the fact that it believes Chinese people were the first to discover the SCS islands and they occupied the islands during the Han Dynasty. To support these claims, China uses maps that were drawn nearly two thousand years ago, which show the Spratly Islands as a part of its territory. In addition to the maps, there also have been several artifacts discovered on the islands that indicate the presence of Chinese fisherman. A British survey ship's "discovery" of Chinese fisherman from the Hainan Province in 1867 supports this argument. The British noted that these men were Chinese nationals and had been working the area's plentiful fishing grounds for some time.[8]

In the late 1940s, the Chinese produced a map that detailed its claims to the territory. This map, known as the nine-dotted line, includes all of the islands in the SCS and the island of Taiwan. China views these areas as critical to its national interests, and its government has been pushing hard to pursue its claims.[9]

In recent years, as an effort to assert its sovereignty, China has been developing the Paracel Island area. One of the best examples of this development occurred on Woody Island, where a small town with an airport, museums, and other very basic amenities exist. The island mainly consists of fishermen, military personnel, and a small amount of tourists.[10]

TAIWAN

Taiwan has played an active role in the SCS region for decades. Beginning in 1956, Taiwan has occupied the Itu Aba, or Taiping Island. This island has the distinction of being the only source of fresh water in the Spratly Islands and also has a moderate amount of development for such a small area. The Taiwanese have built an airport, hospital, and a coast guard outpost on the tiny island.[11]

In 1995, Taiwan made an attempt to reach a peaceful resolution to the conflict. President Lee Teng-hui urged nations to cancel individual claims and instead invest in the multinational South China Sea Development Company. The profits from the venture would be used to fund development projects within each of the respective countries. Unfortunately, the nations could not reach an agreement, and the dispute has continued.[12]

Taiwan is in a particularly challenging position because of its relationship with China. As mentioned earlier, Taiwan's claims mirror those of China's and are based off of the same historical claims. However, it would be in Taiwan's interest to let go of its historical claims and strike a joint development deal with other nations in the region. But if Taiwan were to adjust its position, it would undermine China's interest and could, therefore, intensify the already-contentious relationship between the two. Also, Taiwan does not have the funds to militarily enforce any claims to the SCS islands because it has to devote the majority of its defense resources to protecting its homeland from a possible Chinese invasion. As a result, Taiwan has not been a major actor in the SCS conflict.

VIETNAM

Vietnam also claims the entire SCS as a part of its territory. Similar to China, Vietnam seeks to use historical evidence to prove its ownership of the islands. The Hanoi government considers the Spratlys to be a component of its Khanh Hoa Province and has an established government there. The Vietnamese also refer to the region as the Bien Dong (Eastern Sea) and the Spratly Islands as Truong Sa. Vietnam's strong beliefs in its rights to the sea have led it into several military clashes, primarily with China. These confrontations are discussed in further detail later on in this chapter.[13]

MALAYSIA

Malaysia's claims to the SCS are much smaller in scale than the previous three nations. Malaysia only claims a segment of the Spratly Islands and maintains a small military presence there to protect its interest. Despites its military presence on the island, Malaysia has not initiated violent measures as a resolution to the dispute. On the contrary, Malaysia has sought to solve the problem diplomatically and has pushed for joint economic development plans to be made in the region. Malaysia's largest presence in the SCS can be found on the Swallow Reef. The navy has an outpost there, and there is a runway on the island that allows for the transportation of tourists. The island is also home to a scuba-diving resort.[14]

PHILIPPINES

The Philippines claims a chunk of about fifty small islands within the SCS. The nation believes Thomas Cloma, a Filipino lawyer and businessman who once had aspirations of creating an independent nation named Freedomland on the islands, took ownership of the islands, known in Filipino as the Kalayaans, after Japan was forced to renounce its ownership at the 1951 San Francisco Peace Conference. To protect Cloma's interests, since 1956, the Philippines have maintained a military presence on eight of the islands. In 1974, after being unsuccessful in his bid to gain sovereignty over the area, Cloma transferred the ownership rights to the Philippine government, and in 1978, the president, in a decree, declared the islands were a part of the Philippines.[15]

INDONESIA

Indonesia's interest in the SCS differs somewhat from some of the other nations in the region. Instead of claiming "new" or additional territory, Indonesia is instead trying to protect its already-established boundaries. The area of concern for the Indonesians are the Natuna Islands, which have large reserves of natural gas and a fishing industry that employs the majority of the population. China and Taiwan have both made maritime claims that extend into Indonesia's exclusive economic zone, and the nation is committed to protecting its territorial integrity. [16]

BRUNEI

Similar to Indonesia, Brunei is not looking to expand into the SCS but is simply attempting to protect its EEZ as outlined in UNCLOS. Brunei is the smallest of the major nations involved in the dispute and also one of the closest in proximity to the majority of the islands. The oil and natural gas industry, which accounts for over 50 percent of its GDP and 90 percent of its exports, dominates the country's economy. [17]

These figures demonstrate how important having access to any potential large deposits of oil and natural gas will be for the nation. The area that is of most concern to Brunei is the Louisa Reef because of its proximity to the island and its oil. Malaysia also claims this island, and it has built monuments on the island to support its claims. Brunei is the only nation involved in the dispute that has not built any structures or stationed military personnel in its disputed areas. [18]

CONFLICTS IN THE SOUTH CHINA SEA REGION

Due to the conflicting claims to the SCS and military personnel stationed on the various islands, conflict in the area is inevitable. In most instances, nations have chosen to use diplomatic efforts to solve their differences, however there have been a few cases where diplomacy did not prevent bloodshed.

Sino–Vietnamese Conflict

The majority of the conflicts in the SCS have occurred between China and Vietnam. These nations fought each other for decades on land and even at sea. One of the earliest large-scale naval conflicts between China and Vietnam occurred over the Paracel Islands in January 1974. The islands, known as the Xisha Islands in Chinese and the Hoang Sa Islands in Vietnamese, have changed ownership several times over the course of the last century. For example, the French invaded and occupied the islands in

1938, sparking protest from China and Japan. Japan eventually defeated the French forces and gained control of the islands during World War II. However, after its defeat in the war, Japan renounced its claims to the islands, and China and Vietnam took over various portions.[19]

Establishing who would control which segments of the islands became even more complex during the Indochina Wars and other conflicts in the region. China was constrained in its action because it feared it would spark a larger conflict with the United States. During the 1960s, there were instances when Chinese fishermen were attacked near the Paracel Islands but the Chinese government was unable to respond because Vietnam had the support of U.S. military forces.[20]

As the battles between South Vietnam and its allies and North Vietnam continued, the South began to lose its ability to enforce control over its claimed territory in the SCS. When the United States began to draw down its forces and reduce military assistance, South Vietnam could not defend all of its territories. It withdrew the majority of its troops from the islands, but it still retained its ownership claims.[21]

These ownership claims were tested in January 1974, when Vietnamese and American naval personnel observed two Chinese armored fishing trawlers near Drummond Island. Vietnam and the United States believed the ships were supporting troops who were occupying the area. Also, the Vietnamese government received reports that there were other Chinese military personnel stationed in the area. Saigon sent naval vessels out to sea to order the Chinese to withdrawal, but they declined and then asked the Vietnamese to leave. Both sides refused to leave, making a military showdown an unavoidable reality.[22]

On January 19, 1974, on Duncan Island, Vietnamese troops opened fire on Chinese troops. The Chinese responded, and three Vietnamese soldiers were killed and two others were injured. This standoff sparked a conflict between the two nations that ultimately ended with Vietnam's defeat and China gaining control over all the Paracel Islands. South Vietnam attempted to protest the seizure of the territory in the United Nations, but because China was a member of the Security Council, it was able to block South Vietnam's attempt to raise the issue.[23]

Following the reunification of Vietnam in 1975, the nation reasserted its claim to the Paracel Islands, and its relationship with China continued to deteriorate. The three main factors that sparked Sino–Vietnamese conflict were the perceived mistreatment of Hoa people, who are ethnically Chinese but live in Vietnam; Vietnam's signing of a treaty of friendship with the Soviet Union; and Vietnam's attempts to assert itself in the region. Over the years, the Hoa people had begun to amass a tremendous amount of wealth despite their small population. After the 1976 reunification of Vietnam and the implementation of communist policies, the Hoa had large amounts of their wealth confiscated and redistributed. Some were even required to move from cities to rural areas and forced to engage in farming. As Vietnam's relationship with China continued to sour, some Vietnamese feared that the Hoa would be used as spies, so the Vietnamese government imposed tough measures against them. This treatment angered the Chinese government and was one of the factors that encouraged it to take action.[24]

Arguably, the most significant factor in the decline of Sino–Vietnamese relations was Vietnam's close alliance with the Soviet Union. As Beijing began to reestablish its ties with the United States and separate itself from the Soviet Union, the thought of a staunch Soviet ally being right along its borders proved to be unnerving. In 1978, Vietnam joined the Soviet-dominated Council for Mutual Economic Cooperation (Comecon) and signed the Treaty of Friendship and Cooperation with the Soviet Union. These events sparked China to label Vietnam the "Cuba of the East." It also perceived the treaty between Vietnam and the Soviets as a military alliance that threatened its national interest.[25]

Following these developments, more frequent attacks and incidents began to occur along the two nations' shared boarder. Most of the attacks were small and resulted in very few casualties. The impact of these conflicts changed, however, after the Vietnamese invasion of Cambodia. The invasion led to the ousting of the pro-Chinese Khmer Rouge regime and symbolized Vietnamese ambitions for regional dominance, which China perceived as a major threat. These events became the tipping points for China and sparked its decision to invade Vietnam in order to "teach it a lesson."[26]

The ground-based Chinese attack was launched at dawn on February 17, 1978, and within a day, the Chinese had advanced approximately eight kilometers into Vietnamese territory. At that point, Vietnamese forces began to fight back viciously and were able to slow down the Chinese advances. China also experienced some logistical troubles in getting supplies to its troops during the campaign, which slowed its ability to extend its attacks. Despite its limitations, China continued to launch various attacks over a month-long period. China completed its withdrawal in March 1979 and boasted that it had achieved its established goals even though many analysts view the conflict as a stalemate.[27]

The war caused both China and Vietnam to reassess their military strategies. Vietnam strengthened its ties with the Soviet Union, and the Soviet Union provided it with large amounts of weaponry during the 1980s. Also, Vietnam gave the Soviets access to harbors and allowed it to use certain airfields within Vietnam's territory. Conflicts continued to occur between the two nations, many of them along the borders and, occasionally, some at sea.

One the most notable naval standoffs between Vietnam and China is often referred to as the Johnson South Reef skirmish. This confrontation took place in 1988 and still stands as one of the deadliest encounters in the SCS. The dispute occurred after news spread that China had built a naval observatory on the island. This news angered Vietnam because it claimed the island as a part of its sovereign territory. In response, Vietnam sent troops to plant its national flag on the island and in order to assert more control of the area. China also sent troops out to accomplish the same goal, therefore bringing the nations into direct conflict with each other. China reacted violently to Vietnam's presence and fired on a Vietnamese ship, killing seventy people. As a result of this conflict, China gained control over the majority of the Spratly Islands.[28]

The battles between China and Vietnam have continued even into the twenty-first century. As recently as December 2012, Chinese vessels cut the Vietnamese ship *Binh Minh*'s cables. The ship was conducting a seismic survey forty-three miles southeast of Con Co Island, off Vietnam's Quang Tri Province. The vessel belonged to Petrovietnam, the Vietnamese state-run oil and gas company, resulting in an immediate strong response from the government.

Over the last few years, other similar standoffs have occurred between China and Vietnam. For example, in May 2011, the Vietnamese government also accused Chinese vessels of harassing fishermen and cutting the cables of the *Binh Minh 02* ship while it was doing seismic oil exploration work. Vietnam claimed they were simply searching for oil and gas deposits in its EEZ and were fully within their rights. The Vietnamese Foreign Ministry released video footage showing the Chinese breaking the cables. China defended its actions, citing its right to defend its territory.[29]

As the events over the past few years have shown, China and Vietnam have a fierce rivalry on both land and sea. The adversarial relationship between the two nations has made negotiations very challenging and the threat of armed conflict between the nations a very real possibility. In subsequent chapters, the measures that have been taken to peacefully resolve this rivalry are examined in detail.

Sino–Philippine Rivalry

Initially, the relationship between China and the Philippines was non-adversarial. Each nation had varying claims to the SCS, but they seemed willing to negotiate to resolve the problem. For example, in 1988, then-Philippine-President Corazon Aquino traveled to China to meet with Deng Xiaoping. The two discussed a plethora of economic issues, including the Kalayaan Islands, which the two both staked claims for. During their meeting, Xiaoping made the commitment to stop pushing for Chinese sovereignty on the islands and to instead move forward with a peaceful program of joint development.[30]

There was great hope that these talks would serve as an example for other nations with conflicting claims to the SCS and eventually lead to the stabilization of the region. These hopes were never realized, however, and by the mid-1990s, tension was boiling between China and the Philippines. The spark to the tension occurred in 1994 when the Philippine government approved an oil exploration contract from a U.S. company. The joint venture included Vaalco and its Philippine subsidiary, Alcorn, and they were scheduled to conduct an oil exploration mission near the Reed Bank. China viewed this move not only as an infringement on its sovereignty but also a violation of its joint development and exploration agreement with the Philippines.[31]

In 1995, a set of events occurred that would dramatically alter the nature of the relationship between China and the Philippines. The first was the discovery of Chinese-built structures on Mischief Reef, which was well within the Philippines-claimed EEZ. Additionally, the captain of a Philippine fishing vessel reported that he and members of his crew were held for several days by Chinese authorities on Mischief Reef.[32]

The Filipino government sent out aerial surveillance planes to gauge the extent of Chinese development on the island. The government discovered that the Chinese had built four platforms on stilts, each with three to four bunkers equipped with satellite communication equipment. In addition to the structures, the Chinese also had eight naval vessels near the area. This discovery sparked outrage and caused Philippine President Ramos to call the construction of the structures a blatant violation of international law. In a small show of military force, the Philippines reinforced its garrison on the Kalayaans but failed to get China to remove the bunkers and chose not to make any sort of offensive move against the Chinese.[33]

The Philippines' most favorable option was to negotiate with China instead of engaging in back-and-forth military encounters. In 1995, the nations held two rounds of negotiations, which resulted in both countries developing a code-of-conduct agreement. The code's main aim was to prevent another military standoff from occurring and to increase bilateral cooperation between the two.

Despite its well-meaning intentions, the agreement did not achieve its goals. In January 1996, Chinese and Philippine warships had a small skirmish, and the Philippines received reports that China was upgrading its structures on Mischief Reef. In 1997, more trouble developed when the Philippines discovered even more structures six miles away from the Philippines-controlled Kota Islands and spotted additionally eight more Chinese naval vessels in the area. Also, the Philippine Navy intercepted two vessels that were owned by the Chinese State Oceanic Administration near the Scarborough Shoal. The vessels were carrying Chinese nationals who wished to make a radio broadcast from the island. When confronted, the Chinese stated that the area was within its national territory, but the vessels still withdrew to avoid sparking a larger conflict.[34]

The rivalry between the Philippines and China continues to this day. Even though it has not been as violent as the conflict between China and

Vietnam, it is beginning to become just as significant as the Sino–Vietnamese tensions.

Sino–Indian Rivalry

Although not directly involved in the SCS dispute, India is a major player in the region. Its large population and strong economy allow it to negotiate on nearly equal terms with China. India also has strong, long-standing relationships with other Asian countries who view the nation as a counterbalance to Chinese dominance.

There have been a few military standoffs between China and India over the last few years. In July 2011, the Indian-flagged *INS Airavat* was heading toward Vietnam. When a Chinese radio message warned it to keep out of Chinese waters, it continued on anyway based on its belief that international law was on its side. China also has argued that the exploration activities of India's Oil and Natural Gas Corp (ONGC) around the Paracel Islands were illegal.[35]

As this chapter has shown, the SCS is a complex puzzle composed of the interest of many different nations. Some of the causes of the conflicts are political or military in nature, but evidence has shown that the escalation of the conflict is directly correlated to the prospects of large deposits of oil and natural gas in the region, resources that could greatly alter the nations' economic standing. The next chapter will explore the significance of these resources and the impact they could have on the regional and global economy.

NOTES

1. There are several works that address the growing significance of the economies in Asia. An excellent source for background information on the nations in the region is World Trade Organization, "Trade Patterns and Global Value Chains in East Asia: From Trade in Goods to Trade in Tasks," Geneva, Switzerland, 2011.

2. Brian Morton and Grasham Blackmore, "South China Sea," *Marine Pollution Bulletin*, vol. 42, no. 12, 2001, p. 1236.

3. Leszek Buszynski, "The South China Sea: Oil, Maritime Claims, and U.S.–China Strategic Rivalry," *The Washington Quarterly*, Spring 2012, p. 140.

4. "The Island of Palmas Case," *Permanent Court of Arbitration*, April 4, 1928, [online] www.pca-cpa.org/showfile.asp?fil_id=168. Accessed March 23, 2013.

5. Ibid.

6. "United Nations Convention on the Law of the Sea of 10 December 1982," *United Nations Division of Ocean Affairs and Law of the Sea*, November 9, 2011, [online] http://www.un.org/Depts/los/convention_agreements/convention_overview_convention.htm. Accessed March 24, 2013.

7. Ibid.

8. Michael G. Gallagher, "China's Illusory Threat to the South China Sea," *International Security*, vol. 19, no. 1, Summer 1994, p. 171.

9. Ibid.

10. Ibid.

11. Richard E. Hull, "The South China Sea: Future Source of Prosperity or Conflict in South East Asia?" *National Defense University, Strategic Forum*, no. 60, February 1996, p. 2; Andrew Ring, "A U.S. South China Sea Perspective: Just over the Horizon," *Weatherhead Center for International Affairs*, July 4, 2012, pp. 27, 28.

12. Ring, pp. 27, 28.

13. Gallagher, p. 173; Ring, pp. 23–27.

14. Ring, pp. 14–15.

15. Ian James Storey, "Creeping Assertiveness: China, the Philippines and the South China Sea Dispute," *Contemporary Southeast Asia*, vol. 21, no. 1, April 1999, p. 96.

16. David Rosenberg, "Why a South China Sea Website," *The South China Sea*, 2010, [online] http://www.southchinasea.org/why-a-south-china-sea-website-an-introductory-essay. Accessed May 31, 2013. See especially "Table 5: Territorial Claims in the Spratly and Paracel Islands" on this site.

17. Ring, pp. 16–18.

18. Ibid.

19. Gallagher, p. 172–74.

20. "A Country Study: Vietnam," *Library of Congress Country Studies*, March 22, 2011, [online] http://lcweb2.loc.gov/frd/cs/vntoc.html. Accessed, March 24, 2013.

21. Ibid.

22. Gallagher, p. 172;"A Country Study: Vietnam."

23. "A Country Study: Vietnam."

24. Ibid.

25. Ibid.

26. Ring, pp. 27, 28.

27. Ibid.

28. Hull, p. 2.

29. Alex Watts, "Tensions Rise as Vietnam Accuses China of Sabotage," *Sydney Morning Herald*, June 2, 2011, [online] http://www.smh.com.au/world/tensions-rise-as-vietnam-accuseschina-of-sabotage-20110601-1fgno.html. Accessed May 31, 2013.

30. Storey, p. 96.

31. Ibid, p. 97.

32. Ibid.

33. Ibid.

34. Ibid, p. 98.

35. Tom Page, "India Faces Standoff with China on Sea Oil," *Wall Street Journal*, September 23, 2011, [online] http://online.wsj.com/article/SB10001424053111904563904576586620948411618.html. Accessed March 24, 2013.

TWO

The South China Sea and the Global Oil and Natural Gas Industry

Many of the world's strongest and fastest-growing economies are found on the Asian continent, and several multinational corporations have been taking advantage of this change. For example, over the course of the last few decades, western companies have shifted their manufacturing bases to the region in order to take advantage of the cheap labor and low production costs. These large-scale foreign investments have created millions of jobs and dramatically transformed the standard of living in these nations. The downside to this influx, however, is that increases in manufacturing have caused a major strain on global energy supplies. The Asian continent is by far the world's largest consumer of oil, and it expects its demand to rise sharply over the next few decades. This rapid increase in energy usage has caused the continent to have the world's second-highest-ranked oil supply deficit because its consumption strongly outpaces its supply of energy sources. In order to sustain this economic growth, each country in the region will need a steady and reliable supply of energy.[1]

This dire energy need has made the rich, untapped energy resources of the South China Sea (SCS) an extremely attractive solution. As of now, most Asian countries are importing large amounts of energy products from extremely volatile areas in Africa and the Middle East. The SCS is viewed as a potentially safer and lucrative alternative source. Several foreign firms have strong interest in drilling in the SCS but have been hesitant to do so because of the political uncertainty. This chapter examines the scale of the oil and natural gas reserves in the SCS, the energy industries in each of the claimant nations, and the impact that this new supply of energy could have on global energy markets.

SOUTH CHINA SEA ENERGY DEPOSITS

Scholars must preface any analysis of the energy supplies in the SCS by stating that there are many unknown variables in the equation. The nations in the region have been battling for decades over ownership, and companies that have made attempts to accurately and authoritatively assess the amount of oil and natural gas in the region have received serious opposition. For example, during several cases of oil exploration, people have been detained and vehicles have been attacked or seized. Few companies have been willing to expend the type of capital needed to properly explore the area because they do not have assurance that they will eventually be able to commercially market the products they discover. [2]

However, companies have maintained an interest in exploring because they believe the SCS is home to a large supply of resources. For example, the Energy Information Agency (EIA) estimates that islands in the SCS contain approximately 11 billion barrels (bbl) of oil reserves and 190 trillion cubic feet of natural gas reserves. Other agencies, such as Wood Mackenzie, an energy research and consulting firm, give a much more conservative estimate of 2.5 bbl of oil. The U.S. Geological Survey (USGS) estimates that there may be anywhere between 5 and 22 bbl of oil and between 70 and 290 trillion cubic feet of natural gas that have yet to be discovered. Also, a study conducted by the Chinese National Offshore Oil Company (CNOOC) in December 2012 estimates that there could be up to 125 billion bbl of oil and 500 trillion cubic feet of natural gas. These figures are much larger than those projected by other nations and provide a possible insight into why China has been relentless in its claims to the sea. [3]

SPRATLY ISLANDS

There are also conflicting estimates concerning the amount of hydrocarbon resources in the Spratly Islands. The USGS estimates that there could possibly be between .8 and 12 bbl of oil and 7.5 and 55.1 trillion cubic feet of natural gas in the islands. The majority of these resources are found near the Reed Bank, an area that has been claimed by China, Taiwan, and Vietnam, although the Philippine government discovered natural gas on the bank in 1976. Since its discovery, both an American and a British company have held concessions in the area, but China has been able to block any major abstraction efforts from occurring because of its claim to the area. [4]

PARACEL ISLANDS

In stark contrast to the Spratly Islands, people do not believe the Paracels have any reserves of oil and natural gas. In the absence of economic motivations for conflict, the dispute over the Paracel Islands is largely motivated by its location near strategic shipping lanes and plentiful fishing grounds and the fact that whoever stakes claims to the area can stake claim to an exclusive economic zone (EEZ) that will encompass more valuable islands.[5]

MALAYSIA

Malaysia has experienced rapid economic growth over the last few decades and is now a solidified middle-income nation. The nation produces over 600,000 bbl of oil a day and exports 236,000. Its energy sector is vibrant and on pace to experience strong growth over the next few years. In January 2013, the oil exploration company Petronas announced that it had made the first onshore discovery of oil in the country in twenty-four years. The site, located in the Adong Kecil Wet-1 area, has enormous potential for development.[6]

Petronas also has announced plans to invest fifty-nine billion dollars to purchase equipment in an effort to increase its domestic production capabilities. Malaysia is also making efforts to increase its supply of natural gas. Malaysia and Thailand have a joint development area and are working with some western multinational oil companies to increase the natural gas supply. Malaysia predicts that production will increase annually by 3.3 percent, while it expects domestic consumption to grow at an average of 4.7 percent.[7]

This supply-and-demand gap has caused the government to ramp up its efforts to increase its production. For example, Petronas recently expanded its liquid natural gas (LNG) facilities in Bintulu, making it the world's largest. It currently provides 12 percent of the world's LNG exports at approximately thirty-two billion cubic meters (bcm). With major projects such as this and other investments, Malaysia expects to receive more than twenty billion dollars in export revenue from oil and natural gas.[8]

Operations of Major Oil Companies in Malaysia

Petronas

Petronas, one of the world's largest corporations, is the largest energy firm in Malaysia and is a wholly state-owned enterprise. Petronas holds exclusive ownership rights to all exploration and production projects in

the nation, and all foreign and private companies must form joint agreements with them to operate within the country. In addition to its exclusive production rights in Malaysia, it also has global operations in Asia,
Africa, Australia, Europe, and North and South America. In December
2012, it completed a five-billion-dollar acquisition of the Canadian firm
Progress Energy in an effort to strengthen its position in the North
American energy market.[9]

The company saw a reduction in its profitability due to the halting of
production at one of its facilities in South Sudan, which had traditionally
produced 120,000 bbl a day. Even with this reduction in profit, Petronas
is the largest single source of funding for the Malaysian government. In
2012, it provided an estimated eight billion dollars in revenue. Even
though the company's success is critical to the fiscal prosperity of the
nation, it is not a complete monopoly. It currently accounts for two thirds
of the country's oil and gas production and 60 percent of the nation's
refining capability, leaving opportunity for foreign and privately owned
Malaysian firms to profit.[10]

Exxon Mobile

Exxon Mobile is the largest foreign-owned energy producer in Malaysia. It has partial ownership in six production-sharing contracts and operates forty offshore platforms in seventeen fields in the SCS. It either operates or holds interest in 78 percent to 80 percent of the Satellite Field
Development's remote oil fields in conjunction with Petronas. The company plans to develop a natural gas production hub in the country.[11]

Shell

Shell has been operating in Malaysia since 1910 and has invested approximately eighteen billion dollars in the country throughout this timeframe. The company's main production comes from its offshore operations at Sarawak and Sabah, where it has varying ownership interests.
Also, Shell has proposed to make several large-scale infrastructure investments. For example, in 2011, Shell committed to investing 1.6 billion
dollars to expand existing upstream, midstream, and downstream energy
facilities. It also is investing 250 million dollars to construct a new diesel
processing plant at Port Dickinson. Additionally, Shell has more than
nine hundred retail stations spread across the nation.[12]

Conoco Phillips

Conoco Phillips is another international player in the Malaysian energy market. The company commenced its upstream involvement in 2000,
and currently, it has a large stake in the nation's refineries. Conoco has a
47-percent interest in the Melaka II refinery, which nets the company

approximately 76,000 bbl a day in production. It also has ownership interest in three deep-water blocks off the state of Sabah that are in various stages of development.[13]

Murphy Oil

Murphy Oil is the largest independent operator in the Malaysian market. It has been operating in the country since 1999 and has stakes in and operates six different production-sharing contracts. The company views Malaysia as its most productive investment and has divested in the United States and United Kingdom to concentrate its assets here. Murphy Oil's goal is to have an upstream production of 260,000 bbl per day, and it expects 28 percent of that to come from its Malaysian investments.[14]

PHILIPPINES

Similar to other countries on the Asian continent, the Philippines has a rapidly growing economy with an increasing appetite for sources of energy. Unlike other nations, however, the Philippines does not have a large supply of domestic energy resources. The country has approximately 138 million bbl of proven oil reserves and 98 billion cubic feet of natural gas. The country only produces 26,640 bbl of oil a day and imports 176,000. One positive development is that proven oil reserves are expected to increase to 146 million by 2017. Even with this increase, however, the country will fall far short of its domestic needs.[15]

The one source for possible expansion of the Philippine energy industry is offshore drilling. According to a research project conducted by Brigadier General Eldon G. Nemenzo, the Philippines has 26.3 trillion dollars' worth of energy resources within its EEZ in the Kalayaan Islands. The country has been unable to fully exploit these resources because of the continuous political disputes over the ownership of the SCS. Even with these bleak prospects, several domestic and international energy firms have a stake in the Philippine market because of the potential large profits that could be made if a peaceful settlement was reached.[16]

Operations of Major Oil Firms in the Philippines

Philippine National Oil Company (PNOC)

PNOC is a government-run holding company that has subsidiaries operating in each sector of the oil and natural gas industry. It was established in 1976 and has been the leading actor in the country's energy sector since its inception. The company is currently looking to raise capital to expand its operations by offering a small portion of its shares to the public. PNOC is also planning to construct two coal-fired plants, which will cost an estimated 400 million dollars. [17]

Petron

Petron is the Philippines' largest oil refining and marketing company. It supplies 40 percent of the country's oil requirements and operates an integrated crude oil refinery and petrochemicals complex in the Bataan Province, with a rated production capacity of 180,000 barrels per day. The plant processes crude oil into a full range of petroleum products, including gasoline, diesel, liquefied petroleum gas (LPG), jet fuel, kerosene, industrial fuel oil, and petrochemical feedstock—benzene, toluene, mixed xylene, and propylene. [18]

In addition to its large production operations, Petron also has the largest energy retail network in the country. Petron owns and operates more than two thousand service stations across the Philippines. The company spent 588 million dollars in 2011 to expand and strengthen its operations and compete with the growing level of competition that has followed deregulation of the industry. As of 2011, Petron was still the leading company in the industry, with a 38-percent market share. [19]

Shell

Shell is one of the longest-standing energy companies in the Philippines. It has been in operation since 1914 and has a stake in every aspect of the country's energy sector through its two main subsidiaries: Shell Philippines Exploration (SPEX) and Pilipinas Shell Petroleum (PSP). SPEX was part of a joint venture that discovered the Malampaya gas field, which people believe contains up to seventy-four bcm of natural gas. The company also operates and holds a 45-percent stake in the 4.5-billion-U.S.-dollar Malampaya gas-to-power development. This project is expected to fire three power plants for twenty years once completed. Shell also holds 55 percent in the SC60 license that it shares with Chevron and PNOC. This project is the country's largest single investment in its history and demonstrates Shell's commitment to the Philippines. [20]

Chevron

Chevron is another American-based company that is active in the Philippines. Its business activities include both downstream and upstream investments. It controls 24 percent of the petroleum retail market through its 850 Caltex retail stores. They are a major supplier of jet fuel to international and domestic airlines at the Ninoy Aquino International Airport, and Chevron owns 45 percent of the Malampaya project. [21]

Over the past decade, Chevron has been shifting its strategy in the Philippines. In 2003, it closed its Batanga refinery after forty-nine years of operation and converted it into an oil product import terminal. It acquired the Union Oil Company of California (UNOCAL) in 2005 and is currently looking to open about one hundred more Caltex fuel pump stations in the Philippines within the next five years. The company is also getting involved in the renewable energy business by investing in geothermal plants. These and several other developments show the importance of the Philippines to Chevron.[22]

Nido Petroleum

Australian Nido Petroleum is another international firm with interest in the Philippines. Its most significant investment in the country is its 22.88 percent interest in the Galoc field. Nido plans to drill two horizontal development wells in the oil field with the hopes that they will increase the company's output from 5,600 bbl per day to 12,000 per day. The company is looking to aggressively expand its operations in the Philippines and Southeast Asia over the next few years.[23]

TAIWAN

Taiwan has virtually no domestic sources of energy. The nation only produces a mere five hundred barrels of oil per day and consumes nearly one million. The nation is almost totally dependent on imports for its economic survival, and this dependence places a tremendous amount of pressure on the government. The country imports the majority of its oil from the Persian Gulf and purchases an increasing amount from Angola and countries in West Africa. Also, Taiwan plans to import an estimated 16.8 bcm of LNG in 2013, and Indonesia and Malaysia are its top two suppliers. The nation has also signed new deals with suppliers in Australia, Qatar, and Papua New Guinea. In November 2010, *Business Week* reported that the chairman of Taiwanese state oil and gas firm Chinese Petroleum Corporation (CPC) stated that the country's gas consumption could rise by 45 percent by 2025.[24]

Taiwan is also planning a major increase in its biodiesel use in order to cut reliance on energy imports and reduce the emissions of harmful gases. Researchers estimate that biodiesel use had risen to 630,000 bbl in 2010 after policies were developed to ensure that all diesel fuel sold at filling stations contain at least 1 percent biofuel. Taiwan is also looking to improve its tense relationship with China, engage in several joint development projects, and increase crude oil refining. Taiwan's rapidly growing economy and its nonexistent sources of domestic energy make it a necessity for the government to carefully craft policies that ensure a steady supply of energy.[25]

Operations of Major Oil Firms in Taiwan

Chinese Petroleum Corporation (CPC)

CPC was established in 1946 in Shanghai and relocated to Taiwan after the communist revolution that occurred on the mainland. CPC is a state-owned entity that dominates all segments of the energy industry. It operates several gas fields in the western portion of the nation and has carried out offshore exploration projects. CPC has three main refining operations: Kaohsiung, Dalin, and Taoyuan, which in total account for 720,000 bbl per day. CPC is the main supplier of 70 percent of the nation's service stations and directly operates 645 of those stations.[26]

CPC plans to invest 1.18 billion dollars every year until 2016 in order to acquire overseas energy assets. Out of this total investment, the company will annually spend 1.04 billion dollars on the acquisition of oil and gas fields, primarily in the Asia Pacific region and in Africa. Other places of interest to the company include Brazil, Indonesia, Peru, the United States, Canada, Australia, Malaysia, and Venezuela. CPC also has plans to diversify its energy supplies. It currently acquires 65 percent of its energy supplies from Middle Eastern sources and would like to reduce that dramatically. These and other steps are a part of the company's plan to increase its profits.[27]

Formosa Petrochemical Corporation (FPCC)

FPCC was founded in 1992 in order to take charge of the construction and servicing of Taiwan's first and only privately owned oil refinery, naphtha cracking plant, and cogeneration plant at the No.6 Naphtha Cracker Project. It is Taiwan's largest private enterprise, incorporating more than twenty group companies operating in Taiwan, the United States, China, and Indonesia. The Naphtha Cracker Project has investments in a broad range of industrial interests, including oil refining; petrochemicals; plastic raw materials; secondary processing of plastics, fibers, and textiles; electronic materials; machinery; and transportation.[28]

BRUNEI

The sultanate of Brunei is a small nation whose economy is largely driven by its energy industry. Exploration for oil in the nation began over a century ago in 1899, when the first major discovery occurred in the Seria, Belait, coastal strip. By the 1990s, this area had produced over a billion barrels of oil and was the benchmark for the nation's energy industry. As technology has advanced, however, other areas have become even more viable sources. For example, the Champion offshore oil fields hold nearly 40 percent of the nation's reserves and are currently the nation's most productive area, producing approximately one hundred thousand bbl of oil per day. Another significant offshore oil field is the Magpie, which produces approximately six thousand bbl per day.[29]

In addition, crude oil and gas production account for nearly half of Brunei's GDP and 90 percent of its export revenue. The country also has the distinction of self-sufficiency in energy production and is a net exporter. Brunei exports approximately 141,000 barrels of crude oil a day, and its main costumers are Japan, South Korea, and Australia. The nation also exports over eight bcm of natural gas on an annual basis. The energy sector is one of the largest employers in Brunei, and its prosperity is one of the main reasons Brunei has one of the highest per-capita incomes in Asia.[30]

Operations of Major Energy Firms in Brunei

Brunei Shell Petroleum (BSP)

BSP is the most dominant company in Brunei's energy market and until recently had very little competition in the energy sector. Its main activities are exploration and production of oil and natural gas from onshore and offshore fields. It has an extensive land- and offshore-based energy infrastructure that includes 200 offshore structures and 2,000 km of pipelines, which recover oil and gas from 4,500 reservoirs. It also owns Brunei's only refinery. The company employs 3,500 people and supports an additional 8,000 through its contractors. BSP contributes roughly 90 percent of the nation's oil and gas revenues and continues to be a major player in the industry.[31]

Brunei National Petroleum Company Sendirian Berhad (Petroleum Brunei)

Petroleum Brunei is a wholly government-owned energy company that was established in 2002. Its creation was inspired by other countries in the region (e.g., Malaysia) that have successful national oil companies. Petroleum Brunei owns all mineral rights in 8 prime petroleum blocks spanning an area of approximately 20,552 sq. km. The company is still in its early stages of operation and is spearheading an effort to bring a more competitive environment to the nation's energy sector.[32]

VIETNAM

Over the last decade, Vietnam has been experiencing strong economic growth as a result of its transition to a more market-based economy and large foreign investments. Similar to some of the previously examined countries, this growth has caused a huge spike in domestic consumption, challenging the nation's energy sector. Recently, Vietnam's oil reserve estimates dramatically increased due to large offshore oil discoveries in the Cuu Long and Nam Con Son Basins. Factoring in these new finds, researchers have adjusted Vietnam's proven crude oil reserves to 4.7 billion barrels of proven crude oil and 699 bcm of natural gas reserves. The country currently produces 318,000 barrels of oil per day and exports 267,000 of those.[33]

Vietnam expects to increase its refining production as a result of two newly constructed refineries: Nghi Son and Vung Ro. They currently have the capacity to refine 140,000 barrels a day, and Vietnam expects that number to increase to 340,000 by 2017. The main impediment to Vietnam's energy sector's growth is the SCS dispute. As outlined in the previous chapter, Vietnam has claims to large segments of the sea that contain large quantities of oil and gas. Vietnamese and international companies have not been able to take advantage of these claims because of the risk associated with operating in the restricted territory.[34]

Operations of Major Oil Firms in Vietnam

Petrovietnam

Petrovietnam is Vietnam's government-owned oil company. The company accounts for 20 percent of the oil and 50 percent of the nation's gas production. Petrovietnam also has several joint ventures with international firms. One of the most prominent is Vietsovpetro, a joint venture between Petrovietnam and Russia's JSC Zarubezhneft. Russia is one of Vietnam's closest partners in its energy sector; both countries have several joint development projects. Vietsovpetro produces nearly a third of the country's crude production from its operations in the Bach Ho field in Block 09-3, as well as in Blocks 09-1 and 05-2: sites of the White Tiger, Dragon, and Dai Hung fields.[35]

The company also has agreements with Japanese and South Korean firms that will assist it in further expanding its operations. In April 2012, Petrovietnam announced that it had signed a memorandum of understanding with South Korea's SK Holdings, which allowed the firm to join Petrovietnam's energy projects. The two countries plan to collaborate on several projects, including the building of coal-fired power plants as well as oil exploration, production, and oil processing. There also are thoughts that the company may be making moves toward privatization because recently it has sold several of its subsidiaries. In actuality, the company plans to go private because the increased openness of the industry is sure to spark investment and ultimately increase the productivity of the nation's energy sector.[36]

TNK-BP

TNK-BP is one of Russia's largest oil companies and globally is also one of the top ten privately owned oil producers. The company took over BP's operations in Vietnam and was poised to become a major player in the Vietnamese energy industry until it was acquired by Rosneft, Russia's top crude producer. This acquisition leaves question marks about the fate of TNK-BP's operations in the country, but as of this writing, the company has not made any major shifts in its focus. [37]

Petronas Vietnam

Petronas is Malaysia's national oil company and one of the largest corporations in the world. A significant amount of its investments are found within Vietnam, and evidence shows that this trend will continue in the future. Petronas currently operates four blocks in the country and has interests in nine others. The company also owns two LPG factories in Hai Phong and Dong Nai, in addition to its 93.1-percent interest in Phu My Plastics and Chemical. These investments are in line with the company's stated objective: increasing its production capabilities. [38]

Zarubezhneft

Zarubezhneft was the first foreign company to operate in Vietnam following the nation's entry into the Soviet trading bloc COMECON. It was formed in 1981 through a 50:50 joint venture with Vietsovpetro and became a limited company in January 2011. Zarubezhneft is active in the operation of seven fields in the SCS. Zarubezhneft is also a majority partner in VRJ Petroleum, which it shares with Petrovietnam and Japan's Idemitsu Kosan. [39]

CHINA

One of the most prominent stories of the twenty-first century will be China's dramatic rise to global prominence. The nation, with its population of over one billion people and its exploding industrial base, has developed an insatiable appetite for oil. From the 1950s until 1993, China was self-sufficient in its oil production because it had discovered large amounts of oil in the Daqing oil fields. The Daqing fields are the largest in the nation and are still very productive, but they have failed to keep up with demand. The nation's consistent track record of double-digit growth rates makes acquiring new sources of energy mandatory for its continued prosperity. [40]

China's "oil diplomacy," or its diplomatic moves to secure steady supplies of oil, has forced the country to explore acquiring sources of energy from some of the world's most troubling places. China has been accused of supporting rouge dictators who have been reprimanded by the international community in order to protect its access to those nations' oil. For example, when the leaders of Sudan were under fire for their role in the genocide that took place from 2004 to 2007 in its Darfur region, China was accused by the international community of providing arms and financing to the Sudanese government in an effort to protect its interest in the nation's oil fields. This along with the multitude of other investments China has in very troubled portions of the world have pushed the nation to acquire closer and less risky investments in the SCS.[41]

China currently possesses 14.7 bbl of proven oil reserves and 3.1 trillion cubic feet of natural gas. The nation produces 4 million bbl a day and imports 5 million. Currently, China is the world's second-largest consumer of oil, and it expects to increase to number one in the next few decades. This rapidly increasing demand has forced China to not only seek additional sources of energy abroad but also to maximize its domestic supplies.[42]

Operations of Major Energy Firms

The oil and gas industry in China is dominated by three government-owned corporations: Chinese National Petroleum Corporation (CNPC), China Petroleum and Chemical Corporation (Sinopec), and China National Offshore Oil Corporation (CNOOC). These companies operate within China and across the globe and are responsible for feeding the nation's growing demands. Following, the operations and production capabilities of each of the three are explained.

Chinese National Petroleum Corporation

CNPC was established in 1988 and has developed into a major energy company with both upstream and downstream interest. The company is also involved in logistics, manufacturing, and managing of technical services for energy development projects. In 2010, the company's domestic crude oil production was 2.1 million barrels a day and 72.5 bcm of gas annually. CNPC also has extensive overseas operations and is internationally listed on stock exchanges under its subsidiary, PetroChina.[43]

China Petroleum and Chemical Corporation

Similar to CNPC, Sinopec was established in the 1980s from the assets of the former Ministry of Petroleum Industry. The company operates in four main areas: oil production, refining, sales, and petrochemicals. In 2010, Sinopec produced 850,000 barrels of oil per day domestically and 350,000 overseas. It also produced 12.5 bcm of natural gas. Sinopec is listed internationally through its subsidiary, China Petroleum and Chemical Corporation.[44]

China National Offshore Oil Corp

CNOOC is the third-largest oil company in China and was established to exploit its offshore oil and gas resources. The company is the nation's main operator in the SCS, and in 2010, it was producing 800,000 barrels of crude oil per day domestically and an additional 200,000 overseas. In addition, it also produced nearly 10 bcm of gas domestically and an additional 5 overseas. Its subsidiary, Chinese Oilfield Services, is listed on international stock exchanges.[45]

SCS AND THE GLOBAL OIL INDUSTRY

As this chapter has shown, Asia is one of the dominant players in the global energy market. Nearly every country in the region is projected to have steady growth in its demand for fuels, and virtually none has the ability to meet this demand at the present time. Asia currently has the second-largest energy supply and demand gap and could quickly grow to number one if serious measures are not taken.

This dire situation has not only impacted each of these respective nations' domestic energy policies but also the global energy industry. There currently is a major scramble for any available oil fields across the world. Many countries have been forced into doing business with rogue regimes in order to ensure they continue to have an adequate supply of oil in the future.

The resources in the SCS represent an incredible opportunity to relieve global energy demands. If the nations in the region are able to find a way to equitably exploit the resources, they would be able to at least slow the need for massive expenditures on far and, in some instances, dangerous sources of energy. In the long term, however, it is unlikely that the resources of the SCS will be a long-term solution to each nation's energy needs. Also, nations such as China have demands for oil that differ so much from some of the smaller nations in the region that they face the challenge of negotiating a settlement that is equitable for all parties. The principle reason for the difference is the varying levels of economic development that each country is pursuing. The countries' economic goals are discussed in the next chapter.

NOTES

1. "South China Sea," *U.S. Energy Information Agency*, February 7, 2013, p. 1, [online]   http://www.eia.gov/countries/analysisbriefs/South_China_Sea/south_china_sea.pdf. Accessed June 1, 2013.

2. Alex Watts, "Tensions Rise as Vietnam Accuses China of Sabotage," *Sydney Morning Herald*, June 2, 2011, [online] http://www.smh.com.au/world/tensions-rise-as-vietnam-accuseschina-of-sabotage-20110601-1fgno.html. Accessed May 31, 2013.

3. "South China Sea," pp. 1–13

4. Ibid.

5. Ibid.

6. Central Intelligence Agency, " Malaysia," *World Factbook*, 2013, [online] https://www.cia.gov/library/publications/the-world-factbook/geos/my.html.   Accessed, March 29, 2013;"Malaysia Oil and Gas Report Q3 2013," *Business Monitor International*, February 2013, pp. 9–21.

7. "Malaysia Oil and Gas Report," pp. 9–21.

8. Ibid.

9. Chong Pooi Kon and Barry Porter, "Petronas to Complete C 5.2 Billion Progress Deal This Week," *Bloomberg*, December 9, 2012, [online] http://article.wn.com/view/2013/03/07/Malaysias_Petronas_Says_Profit_Down_14_Percent_6/#/related_news. Accessed August 28, 2013.

10. "Petronas' Annual Profit Down 17%," *Today*, March 7, 2013, [online] http://www.todayonline.com/business/petronas-annual-profit-down-17. Accessed March 30, 2013.

11. "Malaysia Oil and Gas Report," pp. 50–72.

12. Ibid.

13. Ibid.

14. Ibid.

15. Central Intelligence Agency, "Philippines," *World Factbook*, 2013, [online] https://www.cia.gov/library/publications/the-world-factbook/geos/rp.html. Accessed, March 29, 2013.

16. "Philippines Oil and Gas Report Q3 2013," *Business Monitor International*, February 2013, p. 7.

17. Ibid., pp. 54, 55.

18. Ibid.

19. Ibid.

20. Ibid.

21. Ibid.

22. Ibid.

23. Ibid.

24. Central Intelligence Agency, "Taiwan," *World Factbook*, 2013, [online] https://www.cia.gov/library/publications/the-world-factbook/geos/tw.html. Accessed, March 29, 2013; "Taiwan," *U.S. Energy Information Agency*, February 12, 2013, [online] http://www.eia.gov/countries/country-data.cfm?fips=TW. Accessed March 31, 2013.

25. Ibid.

26. "Taiwan Oil and Gas Report Q3 2013," *Business Monitor International*, February 2013, pp. 40–48.

27. Ibid.

28. Ibid.

29. Ibid.

30. Ibid.

31. Ibid.

32. Ibid.

33. "A Country Study: Vietnam," *Library of Congress Country Studies*, March 22, 2011, [online] http://lcweb2.loc.gov/frd/cs/vntoc.html. Accessed, March 24, 2013; Central Intelligence Agency, "Vietnam," *World Factbook*, 2013, [online] https://www.cia.gov/library/publications/the-world-factbook/geos/vm.html.   Accessed, March 29, 2013.

34. Ibid.

35. "Vietnam Oil and Gas Report Q3 2013," *Business Monitor International*, February 2013, pp. 55–68.

36. Ibid.

37. Ibid.;"About TNK-BP," *TNK-BP*, 2013, [online] http://www.tnk-bp.com/en/company. Accessed March 31, 2013.

38. "Vietnam Oil and Gas Report," pp. 55–68.

39. Ibid.

40. Cindy Hurst, "China's Global Quest for Energy," *Institute for the Analysis of Global Security*, January 2007, [online] http://fmso.leavenworth.army.mil/documents/chinasquest0107.pdf. Accessed June 1, 2013; Erica S. Downs, "Who's Afraid of China's Oil Companies?" in *Energy Security: Economics, Politics, Strategy, and Implications*, Jonathan Elkind and Carlos Pacual (eds.), (Washington, DC: Brookings Institute, 2010), [online] http://www.brookings.edu/~/media/research/files/papers/2010/7/china%20oil%20downs/07_china_oil_downs.pdf. Accessed June 1, 2013.

41. "Sudan: A Chronology of Key Events," *BBC News*, March 14, 2013, [online] http://www.bbc.co.uk/news/world-africa-14095300. Accessed March 31, 2013.

42. Central Intelligence Agency, "China," *World Factbook*, 2013, [online] https://www.cia.gov/library/publications/the-world-factbook/geos/ch.html. Accessed, March 29, 2013.

43. "About PetroChina," *PetroChina Company Limited*, 2008, [online] http://www.petrochina.com.cn/Ptr/About_PetroChina/Company_Profile/?COLLCC=589709553&. Accessed April 2, 2013.

44. "About Sinopec," *Sinopec Corp.*, 2011, [online] http://english.sinopec.com/about_sinopec/our_company/6as7tuvr.shtml. Accessed April 2, 2013.

45. "Profile: CNOOC Ltd. (0883.HK)," *Reuters*, n.d., [online] http://in.reuters.com/finance/stocks/companyProfile?symbol=0883.HK. Accessed April 2, 2013.

THREE
Economic Significance of Nations of the South China Sea

Every year, the United States engages in more than a trillion dollars worth of business with nations in the SCS region. These numbers continue to grow annually; in fact, several U.S. corporations, for example, Walmart, Coca-Cola, Dillard's, Target, Sears, J. C. Penney, and Toys "R" Us, have supply chains that rely heavily on Asian manufacturers. Trade with this part of the world is crucial not only for the continued prosperity of the United States but also the global economy as a whole. This chapter analyzes the economic profile of the nations in the SCS region and the impact that a disruption in production levels could have on the U.S. and world economy.

CHINA'S ECONOMY

Over the course of the last few decades, China has become a manufacturing powerhouse and the undisputed economic giant of the Asian continent. It has a GDP of over twelve trillion dollars, and with its economy growing annually at near double-digit rates, research shows it will surpass the United States as the world's largest economy within the next few decades. The United States and China have a nearly inseparable economic relationship: China produces 17 percent of its exports for the U.S. market. This influx of cheap Chinese goods has dramatically altered Americans' standard of living and several of its major retailers' business models.[1]

China and the Walmart Connection

One company in particular that positioned itself to take advantage of Chinese products is Walmart. The company stands as the world's largest retailer with more than three thousand superstores, six hundred discount stores, two hundred neighborhood markets, and six hundred Sam's Clubs in the United States alone. Walmart has become the destination for many Americans because its prices are consistently cheaper than its competitors'. These low prices are made possible by Walmart's strong partnership with Chinese suppliers. Seventy percent of Walmart's goods are made in China, making the company one of the nation's largest trading partners.[2]

Walmart also has a large presence in the Chinese market. The company opened its first Supercenter and Sam's Club in the city of Shenzhen in 1996. Since the opening of its inaugural location, the company has expanded to 390 stores in over 150 cities and 21 provinces. Ninety-nine percent of the store associates are Chinese nationals, and in total, the company employs, directly or indirectly, 100,000 people.[3]

One major difference in Walmart's business model in China and the United States is that, within China, it brands itself as a company that is a major supporter of the local economy. On its website, Walmart states that it uses twenty thousand local suppliers, and 95 percent of its merchandise is sourced locally. Walmart's operation in China differs greatly from its operations in the United States, where foreign products dominate the market.[4]

Coca-Cola and the Chinese Market

Coca-Cola, the world's largest beverage company, also has a significant presence in China. The company commenced its operations in the nation in 1928 and successfully operated there until ties between the United States and China abruptly ended when the nation's communist revolution took place in 1949. Following the normalization of U.S.–Chinese relations, Coca-Cola reestablished its presence in the country in 1979 and has showed steady growth since then.[5]

The company currently operates 35 bottling plants throughout China and in 2004 achieved the milestone of producing its 100 billionth bottle in the country. It is the country's largest beverage company, holding 16 percent of the market share. In addition to Walmart and Coca-Cola, there are several other American companies with large operations in China, and they are reliant upon China for manufactured goods. The Chinese market is crucial for these companies' growth.[6]

Chinese Special Economic Zones (SEZ)

The creation of SEZs has been a crucial component of China's transition to a more market-based economy. The government began to create them in 1980 to attract foreign direct investment (FDI), expand the nation's ports, and create new technologies. The concept initiated with four zones, but after their success, the nation added an additional fifteen. These zones allow foreign companies to operate with more freedom and less regulation from government entities than they normally would. This concept has been very successful, and other nations on the Asian continent have mirrored the model.[7]

TAIWAN'S ECONOMY

Similar to China, Taiwan has created free trade zones to help attract foreign investment. There are currently five free trade zones in the nation: the Port of Keelung, Taipei, Taichung, Kaohsiung, and Taoyuan Air Cargo Park. These zones allow companies to conduct their business operations with limited amounts of restrictive government regulations, and they have helped Taiwan develop a strong economy even though it is a very small nation in terms of its physical size and population.[8]

Taiwan has a national GDP of nearly a trillion dollars and a per-capita income of more than $38,000. Electronics manufacturing for international markets, services, and agricultural endeavors drives its economy. The United States is one of Taiwan's strongest allies and suppliers of aid and also one of its most significant economic partners. In 2012, two-way trade between Taiwan and the United States added up to over 50 billion dollars, and that number will increase in the future.[9]

Taiwan and the Electronics Industry

One of the major drivers of the trade between the United States and Taiwan is the electronics and technology industries. For many years, the United States has marked Taiwan as a major center for technological innovation, and a number of U.S.-based companies have invested billions of dollars in Taiwan's economy. Household names, such as Corning, Microsoft, IBM, and DuPont, are all major foreign investors in the country. These investments have catapulted the Taiwanese electronics industry into one of the world's largest.[10]

Corning Foreign Direct Investment in Taiwan

For the past thirty years, Corning Incorporated has maintained an economic presence in Taiwan. The New York–based company specializes in manufacturing specialty glass products used in televisions, computers, smart phones, and other technology-based products. Videos showcasing the company's products and technologies have become wildly popular on YouTube and gained millions of views. These innovations are due in part to its investments in research and development and manufacturing centers within Taiwan. The company currently has six locations in Taiwan and several others in the East Asian region. [11]

Microsoft Corporation

Microsoft Corporation, the world's largest software provider, also has a strong presence in Taiwan. The company has a Microsoft Technology Center (MTC), a Radio Frequency Identification (RFID) Excellence Center, and a Windows Media Engineering Center based in Taiwan. Taiwan is one of its most strategic locations, and it hopes that, from there, it will be able to make strong penetration into Asian markets. [12]

Other Major U.S. Investors in Taiwan

Corning and Microsoft are merely two examples of American corporate success in Taiwan. Other major investors in Taiwan include Ford Motor Company, Hewlett-Packard for integrated circuit packaging and testing in Taiwan, GTE-Verizon for servers and personal computers, Texas Instruments for semiconductors, and IBM for computers sales and services. [13]

MALAYSIA'S ECONOMY

Malaysia's location along the Straits of Malacca makes the nation one of the most strategically located countries in the world. The waterways in the straits serve as a connection between Asia and the West, and billions of dollars of goods pass through them daily. Also, Malaysia is an emerging economy with ambitions of becoming a contender in the global market for high-technology industries, biotechnology, and other services. The nation currently has a GDP of 492 billion dollars and exports 247 billion dollars worth of goods and services. [14]

The main driver of the country's economy is the energy industry, which is dominated by the state-owned entity Petronas. As mentioned in the previous chapter, Petronas is the largest single source of funding for the government and one of the largest employers in the country. Although the energy sector is a crucial component of the nation's economy, the Malaysian government has been making a conscious effort to ensure it doesn't remain totally reliant upon it. [15]

Malaysia has made several efforts to encourage investments in the high-tech industry and other high-end industries. One innovative strategy the nation created is its Halal Development Corporation, an industry that caters to Muslims. Malaysia is attempting to be the hub of the global Halal industry in order to cater to the world's 1.6 billion Muslims. Statistics show that over the next twenty years, the Islamic population around the globe will grow to more than two billion. This growth will create a tremendous amount of economic opportunity for Halal-compliant companies. [16]

U.S. Corporations in Malaysia

The majority of the American investments in Malaysia fall within the energy sector. As mentioned in the previous chapter, the country has large reserves of oil and natural gas, and several American companies, for example, Conoco Phillips and Exxon Mobile, are deeply invested in the country. In 2012, Conoco Phillips announced plans to invest an additional five billion dollars to enhance its offshore drilling operations off the Sabah Coast. [17]

Motorola Solutions, Inc., has announced plans to expand its investments in Malaysia. The company employs roughly seven thousand people in Malaysia and plans to open a Global Excellence Center in the country in order to provide technical support to its customers. Combined with other efforts in the country, the company is expected to invest approximately one billion dollars. In sum, researchers estimate that the two-way trade between the United States and Malaysia was slightly over forty billion dollars. Due to the foreign companies' continued investments in the country, Malaysia expects these investment numbers to grow dramatically over the next decade. [18]

VIETNAM'S ECONOMY

Over the past few decades, Vietnam has transformed itself from a centrally planned economy to an export-oriented one that attracts billions of dollars in foreign investments. In 2012, the country received 10 billion dollars in FDI and had a GDP of 320 billion dollars. The country exported more than 100 billion dollars' worth of goods in 2012. Vietnam's main export is clothing and apparel, much of which is imported by the United States. In 2011, for instance, Vietnam exported 17.1 billion dollars' worth of goods to the United States, nearly 6 billion dollars in apparel and an additional 2 billion dollars in footwear. Some of America's largest clothing and apparel companies are heavily invested in Vietnam because of its friendly business environment and low production and labor costs. [19]

Nike

America's most popular sports apparel brand, Nike, is heavily invested in the Vietnamese economy. Nike was one of the earliest major American corporations that shifted its operation to Asia in order to take advantage of low production costs. This strategy has been very successful for Nike, and in 2012, the company amassed 24 billion dollars in revenue. In 2010, Vietnam became the company's largest single-country producer, accounting for 40 percent of its footwear production. Nike, the "world's leading innovator in athletic footwear, apparel, equipment and accessories," maintains contracts with factories in Vietnam that manufactured approximately 40 percent of Nike footwear in 2012.[20]

Major corporations view Vietnam not only as a source of production but also as a prospective market for its products. In 2011, GAP Inc. opened its first two stores in Ho Chi Minh City, and then in 2012, it opened stores in Hanoi. The company also plans to open one of its Banana Republic stores in the country. These investments show companies have faith in the future growth and development of the Vietnamese economy.[21]

THE PHILIPPINES' ECONOMY

The economy of the Philippines is experiencing a period of rapid growth. In 2012, its main stock exchange saw a 33-percent increase, and the country believes that in 2013, the exchange will grow by nearly 30 percent again. Since 2008, the market has grown by 294 percent, a growth no other nation has experienced. One of the drivers of this tremendous growth is the confidence in the government's ability to pay its debts and the government's recent announcement that it plans to invest billions of dollars in infrastructure. The Philippines' GDP is more than 423 billion dollars, and it exports approximately 50 billion dollars' worth of goods and services.[22]

Agriculture is one of the main sources of employment in the Philippines; 33 percent of the working population is employed in that sector. The country is the world's largest producer of pineapples and coconuts and also a major producer of rice. The country also has budding financial service and business process outsourcing industries that have attracted large amounts of foreign investment. Several major financial analysis institutions have projected that the Philippines will grow into the one of the world's twenty largest economies within the next few decades.[23]

JPMorgan Chase and Co. and the Philippines

JPMorgan Chase and Co. has had a presence in the Philippines since 1961 and has been one of the major mainstays of the Filipino economy.

The company opened a global service center (GSC) in Manila, which provides support to the various segments of its business. The GSC is open twenty-four hours a day and seven days a week globally and provides support for the operations of card services, retail financial services (home lending, auto finance, education finance, telephone banking, business banking), and treasury and securities services. The GSC also includes such functions as human resources, performance improvement, quality assurance, information technology, accounting, account servicing, collections, operations and operations management, project management, and risk and compliance.[24]

Citigroup and the Philippines

Citi established its first bank in the Philippines in 1902 and is the largest foreign commercial bank in the country. It consistently ranks among the top five commercial banks in terms of profitability and top ten in terms of assets, deposits, and loans. It provides corporate banking, treasury, transactional banking, consumer banking, and trust services. Citi Philippines' Institutional Clients Group is a recognized leader in arranging and providing financial services for the public sector, top-tier Filipino corporates, multinationals, and financial institutions operating in the country. It also provides domestic debt and equity underwriting and financial advisory services through Citicorp Capital Philippines, Inc.[25]

Business Process Outsourcing (BPO)

The Philippines is quickly becoming the world's go-to country for business process outsourcing. Its huge English-speaking population combined with its well-developed technological infrastructure has caused several companies to shift their nonessential duties to the country. In 2013, BPO expects its revenue to increase to 16 billion U.S. dollars and to provide employment for over 900,000 Filipinos.[26]

INDONESIA'S ECONOMY

Indonesia has the largest economy in Southeast Asia and is one of the strongest emerging markets in the world. The country is a member of the G-20, and the West considers it an industrialized nation. Similar to many of the countries in the region, Indonesia has a market economy where government entities play a major role. In 2012, the country had a GDP of slightly over 1 trillion dollars and exported approximately 188 billion dollars' worth of goods and services.[27]

In 2012, the bilateral trade between the United States and Indonesia stood at around 25 billion dollars. Indonesia is a major producer of oil and natural gas, and as mentioned in the previous chapter, several American companies are heavily invested in the country. The revenue generated from the sale of oil and natural gas has helped to create a budding middle class with a strong demand for consumer products.[28]

Proctor and Gamble (P&G)

P&G has identified the country as a one of the most promising markets in its global strategy. In 2011, the company committed to building a 100-million-dollar, 51,000-square-foot diaper-producing factory. It is anticipated that the factory will employ 400 people and produce diapers for the country's large baby population.[29]

General Motors

General Motors also is reestablishing its commitment to Indonesia with the reopening of its plant in West Java. The plant is expected to manufacture 40,000 cars and employ 800 people. GM plans to sell the cars it produces on both the domestic and international markets. It is hoped that Indonesia will serve as a hub for the company's penetration into the Southeast Asian market.[30]

BRUNEI'S ECONOMY

Although Brunei is one of the smallest countries in Southeast Asia, it has a strong economy that has one of the highest per-capita incomes in the world. The nation's economy is largely driven by the energy sector, which accounts for 60 percent of its 21-billion-dollar GDP and 90 percent of its 12 billion in exports. The majority of its exports are destined for resource-hungry nations, such as Japan, South Korea, and Australia. Brunei's ability to export a large percentage of its energy production to neighboring countries makes the economic stability of the region crucial to the nation's success.[31]

The United States and Brunei have a very small economic relationship in comparison to the relationship that other nations in the region have with foreign investors. In 2011, a two-way trade between the two countries stood at slightly over 200 million dollars, a substantial increase from the year before. The U.S. Department of State's investment climate index, however, highly ranks the country because of its stability, openness to foreign investments, and attractive tax incentives.[32]

General Electric (GE)

One large American corporation that is seeking to take advantage of the opportunities in Brunei is GE. In July 2012, the company opened its first office in the capital city of Bandar Seri Begawan. The company has had a presence in Brunei over the last thirty years, but the opening of this office is a demonstration of its efforts to further those initiatives. It is GE's hope that its innovative technologies will help enhance the energy sector in Brunei and also serve as a springboard for its investments in other nations in the region.[33]

There are several other American firms involved in the energy sectors who have a large investment in the country. As the nation begins to shift from its reliance on its natural resources as its sole source of revenue, there certainly will be additional opportunities for foreign investors in various segments of the economy.

REGIONAL ECONOMIC INTEGRATION

There has been a strong emphasis in the last few years to increase economic cooperation among nations in the SCS region. As discussed in this chapter, many of the countries have rapidly growing economies and are looking to expand their markets. Several different organizations have formed and signed agreements with the goal of fostering economic development in the region. Some of those agreements have proven to be controversial.

The Asia-Pacific Economic Cooperation (APEC)

Asian companies formed APEC in 1989 as an informal organization whose aims were to discuss economic issues. Initially, the meetings only took place between representatives on the ministerial level, but over the years, the organization grew in significance. In a 1994 meeting in Indonesia, the organization established the "Bogor Goals," which sought to establish free trade in the Asia-Pacific by 2010. Although the group was unable to accomplish its goal of free trade by 2010, it had made significant progress toward it.[34]

Association of Southeast Asian Nations (ASEAN)

In 1967, Indonesia, Malaysia, the Philippines, Singapore, and Thailand, the five founding members, formed ASEAN. It aimed to resolve economic, social, and cultural issues along with any other problems that plagued the region. The association has continued to grow over the years, achieving many goals, growing its list of member nations, and firmly establishing itself as the premier regional association on the Asian continent.[35]

ASEAN has been able to successfully create free-trade areas among its members. For example, it has convinced various nations to gradually remove import tariffs on a country-specific basis. Specifically, due to AS-EAN's work, Brunei, Indonesia, Malaysia, the Philippines, Singapore, and Thailand have eliminated import duties on 99 percent of imported items. In other member nations, the ASEAN has been moving to eliminate tariffs at a slower pace or have reduced them to an extremely low level.[36]

Regional Comprehensive Economic Partnership (RCEP)

The agreement with the largest potential reached by ASEAN is the RCEP. The deal was created in November 2011 as a compromise between those who favored the East Asia Free Trade Agreement, which only included ASEAN members, China, Japan, and South Korea, and those who preferred the Comprehensive Economic Partnership in East Asia, which added three additional countries: India, Australia, and New Zealand. In total, the agreement connects sixteen different Asia-Pacific countries whose population totals over 3 billion and share a combined GDP of 17 trillion.[37]

The basic principle of the RCEP is to harmonize the region's existing free-trade agreements, promote greater regional economic integration, progressively eliminate barriers to trade, and ensure fairness and consistency within the World Trade Organization's (WTO) rules. The partnership also helps to facilitate trade in services, investments, economic and technical cooperation, intellectual property rights protection, competition, and dispute resolution.[38]

Another significant goal of the partnership is to close the development gap found among nations in the region. The deal seeks to allow smaller nations access to markets in the larger countries and to also shift the foreign investment in the region to a more equitable formula. It is hoped that the partnership will lead to a smooth transition from a foreign-based to a regional-based economy.[39]

In order to gain the buy-in of smaller nations, the RCEP has adopted several rules that allow members to opt out of policies they disagree with and also allows for the protection of sensitive industries that are crucial to the economic stability of certain nations. This flexibility could be an impediment to the functionality of the organization; however, if countries are unwilling to sacrifice individual interest for those of the region, it remains to be seen how this will play out in a contentious situation.[40]

Arguably, the most notable aspect of the RCEP is that it includes China in the deal and excludes the United States. Under the Obama administration, the United States has made Asia a priority and has encouraged U.S.-based corporations to expand into these new markets. The RCEP has stated that it has a flexible agreement that could allow for other nations to join who agree to its principles of engagement. It is still somewhat uncertain how the RCEP could impact the United States' economic interest in the region, but it clearly has the potential to be a major shift in the balance of power.[41]

Trans-Pacific Partnership (TPP)

The TPP is an ambitious trade initiative involving Australia, Brunei, Chile, Malaysia, New Zealand, Peru, Singapore, Vietnam, and the United States. The United States has been the lead actor in the TPP and has been branding the deal as a vehicle that will push its economic interest in the region. The countries in the TPP negotiations made up 31 percent of the U.S. goods and services trade in 2011, and the economies in the Asia-Pacific region in sum makeup 56 percent of U.S. trade.[42]

Japan has also expressed interest in joining the TPP negotiation in order to maintain its relevance in the region's economic outlook. Japanese government officials have estimated that joining the TPP would expand the nation's economy by 33 billion dollars. Some Japanese, however, resist the idea of joining the partnership. The agricultural industry has vocalized its concerns about having a massive influx of U.S. products flood its markers. Also, the nation has expressed concerns and a desire to ensure the protection of its rice industry, but it is unclear, at this point, what the plans are for other segments of the economy. Even with the domestic controversy that the TPP has stirred, the potential of adding another one of the world's largest economies to the TPP could have a tremendous impact of the value of the agreement.[43]

The U.S. already has free-trade agreements in place with Australia, Canada, Chile, Mexico, Peru, and Singapore. These countries account for 85 percent of the U.S.'s trade with countries in the TPP block. The United States also has a significant trade relationship with Malaysia and Vietnam but does not have a free-trade agreement with them. It hopes that the TPP will harmonize trade policies with each of these nations to encourage the establishment of additional investments.[44]

The biggest controversy surrounding the TPP is that it does not include China, the world's second-largest economy and the most dominant nation on the Asian continent. China's absence has angered some, but it also has caused others to see the absence as an opportunity to counter the nation's influence in the region. The organizing countries designed the TPP to bar any country that does not meet certain international standards for business practices from entry. Because of the Chinese government's tight control of its economy, it is difficult for the nation to meet the minimum requirements of partnership. However, since the RCEP is an alternative, there may be very little incentive for China to change its way of doing business. Only time will tell which of these major regional economic integration initiatives will gain the most traction in the region.[45]

CONCLUSION

The information given in the last two chapters has not only shown that the countries involved in the SCS debate have vibrant economies but also that the world is dependent on its productivity. Countless numbers of Western multinationals have large presences and operations across the region, and these companies rely on the Asian market for their growth. The majority of consumer goods people purchase are manufactured on the Asian continent. Manufacturing, combined with the region's ability to avoid the pitfalls of the global financial crisis, has caused many to look at the region as a source of future growth for the global economy. However, this outlook will be jeopardized if any sort of sustained conflict over the SCS occurs, making a resolution even more imperative. Another potential conflict in the region is that the Chinese government has been building up its naval capacity for the past few years. For many years, China had invested very little in its naval forces, but it is rapidly changing its tactics. The next chapter explores in detail the development of Chinese naval forces and its effects on the nation's aspirations for regional and world dominance.

NOTES

1. Central Intelligence Agency, "China," *World Factbook*, 2013, [online] https://www.cia.gov/library/publications/the-world-factbook/geos/ch.html. Accessed March 31, 2013; "The People's Republic of China," *Office of the United States Trade Representative*, n.d., [online] http://www.ustr.gov/countries-regions/china-mongolia-taiwan/peoples-republic-china. Accessed April 2, 2013.

2. "Walmart U.S. Stores," *Walmart*, 2012, [online] http://corporate.walmart.com/our-story/our-stores/united-states-stores. Accessed April 2, 2013.

3. Ibid.

4. "Walmart China Factsheet," *Walmart*, n.d., [online] http://www.wal-martchina.com/english/walmart/index.htm. Accessed April 4, 2013.

5. "Delicious and Delightful New Year," *Coca-Cola History and Coke Memorabilia*, 2010, [online] http://www.7xpub.com/coke-articles-and-essays/1625-delicious-and-delightful-new-year.html. Accessed April 5, 2013; "Coca-Cola Inaugurates US$160 Million Bottling Plant in China Creating 500 Direct Jobs; To Invest US$ 4 Billion over 3 Years," *FDI Tracker*, March 30, 2012, [online] http://www.fditracker.com/2012/03/coca-cola-inaugurates-us160-million.html. Accessed April 7, 2013; "As China Opens Its Doors, Coca-Cola Pours In: Trade: The Soft Drink Maker Is Building More Plants and Has Plans to Reach More of the Nation's Huge Market as Its Economy Strengthens," *Los Angeles Times*, November 8, 1993, [online] http://articles.latimes.com/1993-11-08/business/fi-54690_1_soft-drink. Accessed April 7, 2013.

6. Laurie Burkitt, "China Accuses Coca-Cola of Illegally Using GPS," *Wall Street Journal*, March 13, 2013, [online] http://online.wsj.com/article/SB10001424127887323826704578357131413767460.html. Accessed April 4, 2013.

7. Jin Wang, "The Economic Impact of Special Economic Zones: Evidence from Chinese Municipalities," *London School of Economics*, November 2009.

8. "Introduction to the Enterprises," *Taiwan Free Trade Zone*, 2011, [online] http://taiwan-ftz.com/lp.asp?ctNode=542&ctUnit=206&baseDSD=52&mp=3. Accessed April 7, 2013.

9. Central Intelligence Agency, "Taiwan," *World Factbook*, 2013, [online] https://www.cia.gov/library/publications/the-world-factbook/geos/tw.html. Accessed April 3, 2013.

10. "Investment," *U.S. TaiwanConnect*, 2013, [online] www.ustaiwanconnect.org/US-Taiwan-Relations/Investment. Accessed April 5, 2013.

11. Corning Incorporated, "A Day Made of Glass . . . Made Possible by Corning," *YouTube*, 2011, [online] http://www.youtube.com/watch?v=6Cf7IL_eZ38. Accessed June 2, 2013. This video has received more than twenty million views. More information about the company can be found at its official website, http://www.corning.com/index.aspx.

12. "Microsoft Technology Center: Taipei," *Microsoft*, 2013, [online] http://www.microsoft.com/en-us/mtc/locations/taipei.aspx. Accessed April 7, 2013.

13. "2012 Investment Climate Statement—Taiwan," *U.S. Department of State*, June 2012, [online] http://www.state.gov/e/eb/rls/othr/ics/2012/191245.htm. Accessed April 7, 2013.

14. Central Intelligence Agency, "Malaysia," *World Factbook*, 2013, [online] https://www.cia.gov/library/publications/the-world-factbook/geos/my.html. Accessed April 3, 2013.

15. "Malaysia Oil and Gas Report Q3 2013," *Business Monitor International*, February 2013, pp. 9–21.

16. Malaysia has been an industry leader in the development of Halal certification procedures. For more information, please see the Halal Industry Development Corporation's website, http://www.hdcglobal.com/publisher/alias/?dt.driverAction=RENDER&pc.portletMode=view&pc.windowState=normal&pc.portletId=Newslatest.newsPortlet.

17. Fauziah Ismail, "U.S. Companies Ready to Pump More Money into Malaysia," *New Strait Times*, May 19, 2012, [online] http://www.nst.com.my/top-news/us-companies-ready-to-pump-more-money-into-malaysia-1.85573. Accessed April 5, 2013.

18. "PM U.S. Companies to Invest Billion in the Country," *Star Online*, May 19, 2011, [online] http://thestar.com.my/news/story.asp?file=/2011/5/19/nation/20110519095125&sec=nation. Accessed April 5, 2013; "U.S. Relations with Malaysia," *U.S. Department of State*, October 24, 2012, [online] http://www.state.gov/r/pa/ei/bgn/2777.htm. Accessed June 2, 2013.

19. Central Intelligence Agency, "Vietnam," *World Factbook*, 2013, [online] https://www.cia.gov/library/publications/the-world-factbook/geos/vm.html. Accessed April 3, 2013.

20. "U.S. Apparel Imports from Vietnam Continue to Surge: Up 26%," *American Chamber of Commerce Vietnam*, 2012, [online] http://www.amchamvietnam.com/1779. Accessed March 5, 2013; "Our Mission: To Bring Inspiration and Innovation to Every Athlete in the World," *Nike, Inc.*, 2013, [online] http://nikeinc.com/pages/about-nike-inc. Accessed April 2, 2013; Allan Brettman, "Nike Relies Even More on Vietnam for Shoes, Annual Report Shows," *The Oregonian*, July 25, 2012, [online] http://www.oregonlive.com/playbooks-profits/index.ssf/2012/07/nike_relies_even_more_on_vietn.html. Accessed April 5, 2013.

21. "Gap Inc. Expands in Asia Pacific with First Stores in Vietnam and Guam," *Gap Inc.*, August 22, 2011, [online] http://www.gapinc.com/content/gapinc/html/media/pressrelease/2011/med_pr_VietnamGuam.html. Accessed April 7, 2013; "Gap Inc.'s Global Runway" *Gap Inc.*, November 17, 2011, [online] http://www.gapinc.com/content/dam/gapincsite/documents/GPS_Global_Runway_Backgrounder.pdf. Accessed April 7, 2013.

22. Ian Sayson, "Philippine Stocks to Overtake Economy This Year: Southeast Asia," *Bloomberg News*, March 7, 2013, [online] http://www.bloomberg.com/news/2013-03-06/philippine-stocks-to-overtake-economy-this-year-southeast-asia.html. Accessed June 2, 2013.

23. Central Intelligence Agency, " Philippines," *World Factbook*, 2013, [online] https://www.cia.gov/library/publications/the-world-factbook/geos/rp.html. Accessed April 3, 2013.

24. "Philippines," *J.P.Morgan*, 2013, [online] http://www.jpmorgan.com/pages/jpmorgan/ap/philippines. Accessed April 3, 2013.

25. "Citi in the Philippines," *Citibank Philippines*, 2012, [online] http://www.citibank.com.ph/gcb/footer/aboutus.htm. Accessed June 2, 2013.

26. "Economic Update: The Philippines: BPO's Rising Potential," *Oxford Business Group*, April 24, 2012, [online] http://www.oxfordbusinessgroup.com/economic_updates/philippines-bpo%E2%80%99s-rising-potential. Accessed April 7, 2013.

27. Central Intelligence Agency, " Indonesia," *World Factbook*, 2013, [online] https://www.cia.gov/library/publications/the-world-factbook/geos/bx.html. Accessed April 3, 2013.

28. Ibid.

29. Randal Mah, "Procter and Gamble Takes 100 Million Indonesia Plunge," *Emerging Money*, October 5, 2011, [online] http://emergingmoney.com/consumer/procter-gamble-takes-100-million-indonesia-plunge. Accessed February 12, 2013.

30. Indah Setiawati, "General Motors Indonesia to Produce 40,000 Cars at Bekasi Plant," *Jakarta Post*, August 12, 2011, [online] http://www.thejakartapost.com/news/2011/08/12/general-motors-indonesia-produce-40000-cars-bekasi-plant.html. Accessed June 2, 2013.

31. Central Intelligence Agency, "Brunei," *World Factbook* (2013), [online] https://www.cia.gov/library/publications/the-world-factbook/geos/bx.html. Accessed April 3, 2012.

32. "Brunei Darussalam," *Office of the United States Trade Representative*, n.d., [online] http://www.ustr.gov/countries-regions/southeast-asia-pacific/brunei-darussalam. Accessed April 4, 2013; "2012 Investment Climate Statement—Brunei," *U.S. Department of State*, June 2012, [online] http://www.state.gov/e/eb/rls/othr/ics/2012/191116.htm. Accessed April 5, 2013.

33. Al-Haadi Abu Bakar, "GE Opens Brunei Office," *Brunei Times*, July 1, 2012, [online] http://www.bt.com.bn/business-national/2012/07/01/ge-opens-brunei-office. Accessed April 1, 2013.

34. "History," *Asia-Pacific Economic Cooperation*, 2013, [online] http://www.apec.org/About-Us/About-APEC/History.aspx. Accessed April 3, 2013.

35. "History," Association of Southeast Asian Nations, 2012, [online] http://www.asean.org/asean/about-asean/history. Accessed March 30, 2013.

36. Ibid.

37. Murray Hieber and Liam Hanlon, "ASEAN and Partners Launch Regional Comprehensive Economic Partnership," *Center for Strategic and International Studies*, December 7, 2012, [online] http://csis.org/publication/asean-and-partners-launch-regional-comprehensive-economic-partnership. Accessed April 1, 2013.

38. Ibid.

39. Ibid.

40. Ibid.

41. Jane Perlez, "Asian Nations Plan Trade Bloc That, Unlike U.S.'s, Invites China," *New York Times*, November 20, 2012, [online] http://www.nytimes.com/2012/11/21/world/asia/southeast-asian-nations-announce-trade-bloc-to-rival-us-effort.html. Accessed April 7, 2013.

42. Brock Williams, "Trans-Pacific Partnership (TPP) Countries: Comparative Trade and Economic Analysis," *Congressional Research Service*, January 29, 2013, pp. 1–12.

43. Ibid.

44. Ibid.

45. Ibid.

FOUR

China's Increased Naval Power and Aspirations for Regional Dominance

China has been swiftly modernizing its armed forces and increasing its defense budget by double digits for the past two decades. According to the Stockholm International Peace Research Institute (SIPRI), China's annual defense spending rose from more than 30 billion dollars in 2000 to almost 120 billion in 2010. This expansion has dramatically increased the technological capabilities of its military and has raised concern among countries in the South China Sea region and around the globe.[1]

China's massive population of more than 1.3 billion people gives it an unmatched advantage over nearly every nation in the world because it has access to large manpower, which it can use for combat. Researchers estimate that the nation has more than 600 million males and females who are considered fit for military service. In addition, due to the rapid growth of its population, annually the country adds an additional nineteen million people to the ranks of fighting age. There are several scholarly works that examine the depth and effectiveness of the Chinese military forces as a whole, but this particular chapter focuses solely on the evolution of the People's Liberation Army Navy (PLAN).[2]

CHINESE NAVAL HISTORY

Despite its enormous size and current economic dominance, for many years scholars believed China had no significant naval history. Because the main threat to China's security came from nomadic Central Asian groups, China did not have a major incentive to develop its naval capabilities. More recent studies, however, reveal that China's naval history is nearly as old as that of European nations. The first mention of the Chinese using ships in military operations dates back as early as 1045 B.C., and in the years that followed, China continued to progress with the advent of new technologies. In 960 A.D., during the time of the Song Dynasty, Chinese naval technology continuously created new concepts and outpaced the innovations emanating from European nations.[3]

One distinguishing factor in China was the purpose for which it used the navy. The Chinese built a major hydraulic defense system that patrolled the rivers and canals in the area. These interior maritime-based operations played a crucial role in protecting China from its most immediate adversaries. Over the years, Chinese naval power continued to expand to the point where it was able to project power on neighboring countries.[4]

From 1403 to 1424, China developed a tribute system that involved states in South and Southeastern Asia. These nations saw China as an advanced civilization and were eager to cooperate with it in order to gain some perceived benefits. They believed gaining the Chinese leadership's approval would help them legitimize the succession of their new rulers and grant them Chinese military protection in the case of attacks.[5]

The most significant advantage to collaboration with China was the handsome profits the countries would make through commerce. Trading with China provided nations with access to high-quality goods that they could not obtain in other portions of the world. China's manufacturing comparative advantage allowed it to demand that other nations submit to its request for tributes. The revenue brought in from this system inspired Emperor Yung-lo to attempt to expand the tribute system even further. Yung-lo commissioned seven great expeditions that spanned over nearly twenty years.[6]

The first fleet sailed from 1405 to 1407, with 62 vessels carrying 28,000 men, and reached India, as did the second and third. The forth voyage sailed from 1413 to1415 and reached Aden and the Strait of Hormuz on the Persian Gulf. A fifth voyage also went as far as Aden. The seventh voyage started out with 27,500 men and reached Hormuz again from 1431 to 1433. Chinese vessels visited far down the east coast of Africa, and seven Chinese vessels reached Mecca.[7]

These expeditions were successful in establishing new markets for Chinese goods and in increasing the nation's international political alliances. Leaders of the nations China visited also made trips to China, and those nations believed a prosperous mutually beneficial relationship would ensue. This belief never quite came into fruition, and by 1433, China ended its pursuit of naval power.[8]

The principal reason for the abrupt end to its naval dominance was the expense of continued naval expansion. The nation struggled from the financial pressure caused by costly wars against the Mongols and the construction of the capital city of Beijing. China also proved to be uninterested in colonial possibilities because its major source of revenue came from land tax and not trade. However, the failure to develop itself into a major maritime power proved very costly for China. During the colonial era, such nations as Japan, Portugal, Spain, the Netherlands, Great Britain, and the United States were able to establish themselves in the waters off of the coast of China. China's inability to assert itself from a maritime standpoint would serve as an early wakeup call for the nation.

COMMUNIST REVOLUTION AND TAIWAN

No issue has brought China's naval inadequacies to the forefront more than its long-standing dispute with Taiwan. In the six decades that have passed since the communist revolution that forced the Kuomintang government to flee to Taiwan, neither side has been willing to come to a sovereignty agreement. China desires to reintegrate Taiwan into its territory with a substantial amount of autonomy. Taiwan, however, is not willing to negotiate and has rejected proposals to reunite the two countries. This stance is supported by the majority of the Taiwanese but is a very contentious issue for China. The Chinese government has been actively using its economic leverage to attempt to get nations around the world to remove their recognition of Taiwan as an independent state.[9]

Because the two nations are located in such close proximity to each other and Taiwan is an island, it was inevitable that there would be some sort of major naval offensive between the two to resolve the territorial dispute. To date, several standoffs between China and Taiwan, which are frequently referred to as the Taiwan Strait crises, have taken place (more details about these crises are given later in the chapter). In the 1990s, another major event caused a dramatic shift in the needs of the people of China. As the nation became more and more industrialized, its demand for energy began to outstrip its supply, and in 1993, China began importing oil. Oil importation made secure shipping lanes critical to China's continued economic growth and a strategic priority for the nation. This shift in reality caused various Chinese authors to reflect on how the government should take these new priorities into account and formulate Chinese naval policy.

REFLECTIONS OF CHINESE SCHOLARS

The one issue that practically all scholars agreed upon was the importance of increasing the nation's naval power. They understood that without a strong naval presence, the nation would not be able to sustain its modern economy. However, they disagreed on how to formulate a naval plan. Four main theories emerged from this debate, and each are discussed in the following segment of the chapter.

Defining Naval Power

The scholars first dealt with the issue of defining naval power within the Chinese reality. Some viewed power from a more militaristic standpoint, while others defined it more broadly to include control of resources and the natural environment. There also were some authors who believed that the Chinese reality was so unique that they needed to develop a distinctive definition of maritime power. A professor at China's premier naval academy, Dilian Vessel, Dr. Lu Rude, posed a new definition of Chinese sea power, which included several different categories. Some of the key points within his definition were ensuring that China had a comprehensive maritime education system; skilled maritime technicians; advanced technology and equipment; a powerful navy; oceangoing commercial, fishing, surveying, and engineering fleets; and a solid maritime legal framework and law enforcement.[10]

The War Theories and Strategic Studies Department of the Academy of Military Science stated that China needed to chart its own path and avoid simply copying the definitions of Western countries. The department advocated for the development of a concept of sea power with "Chinese characteristics." This included limiting the goals and range of the policy to focus solely on protecting maritime rights and sovereignty within the parameters established by UNCLOS; safeguarding the use of maritime resources and the safety of China's important overseas interest; and combining military, political, economic, diplomatic, and cultural methods.[11]

Another point of contention in the discussion of China's maritime security was the balance in allocation of resources for land- and sea-based initiatives. Some argued that maritime power was the key to China's future, others made the case that the two were equal in importance, and finally, some held the belief that land power was more significant. Each of these schools of thought had influential authors who wrote a number of scholarly articles supporting their positions. The authors who argued that China needed to increase its naval power essentially gave five main reasons for their stances. The first main reason was because of the nation's growing economic interest in the region. China was importing millions of barrels of oil and natural gas and exporting billions of dollars of goods on a daily basis, all of which traveled through the sea. To compound the issue, most of the waterways that China claims as its territorial waters are currently being exploited by other nations. The second reason was that other nations were calling into question China's territorial integrity because of its inability to firmly establish its maritime boundaries.

The third major reason scholars argued China needed to increase its navy was because they were concerned about traditional security threats from the navies of other nations. Authors have encouraged the government to station military forces around its islands to protect it from attacks. The fourth point the scholars raised was the growing economic interest the nation has developed overseas. Chinese firms have made billions of dollars in investments in various locations across the globe, and some of these locations are extremely volatile. This reality necessitates that China have the ability to rapidly respond with military force if other nations threaten those interests. The fifth and final reason for a strong naval power is to protect Chinese nationals living abroad. With the increasing number of Chinese citizens opening businesses overseas, it is crucial that the nation has the ability to evacuate them in the case of an emergency.

Developing a Sea Consciousness

Another topic Chinese intellects grappled with was the necessity for China to develop a sea consciousness among the Chinese citizenry. They believed accomplishing this task would be particularly challenging in China because of the years its population spent isolated from the outside world. Despite this challenge, the government hoped that with proper education, the citizenry will have a clearer understanding of the importance of the sea and the nation's maritime efforts. The nine key points that Chinese scholars hoped to embed in the population were an understanding of the maritime territory, economy, politics, rights and interest, resources, environment, science and technology, national security, and military space. The broader goal behind creating this consciousness was to make citizens believe that China's expansion from a continental power to a maritime power would be in the nation's best interest.[12]

Naval-Centric or Comprehensive Security Strategy

Scholars also struggled with deciding which agency would play the lead role in securing the maritime environment. Some argued that it should be the navy and that a special emphasis should be placed on modernizing and developing PLAN. Liu Zhenhuan, an official from the Naval Research Institute, stated that although sea power was inclusive of several factors, such as science, technology, economics, and the military, the navy was the most critical component. Other authors who proscribed to this same viewpoint concluded that only with a strong and modern PLAN could China become a prosperous nation.[13]

Even though other authors differed in their opinion of the significance of the PLAN, nearly all agreed that it had a role to play in ensuring the nation's maritime security. They also realized that other agencies could have an even more significant role to play. They advocated for the PLAN to coordinate its efforts with some of these agencies: public security, communications, tax administration, customs, fishing industry, environmental protection, and health departments. Scholars hoped that integrating the efforts of these departments would lead to a more holistic approach to maritime security that would benefit the nation over the long term.[14]

International Law and Cooperation

The fourth issue the writers debated was the role that international law should play and the amount of cooperation that should occur between China and its neighbors to secure its maritime interest. Some authors believed that China should take a nationalistic approach and handle its own issues internally, while others believed that it would be in the nation's best interest to cooperate with neighboring countries. Each side made various arguments to support its position, many having overlapping points.[15]

Those who believed that China should rely on international law called for the strengthening of the nation's maritime law enforcement. They suggested specific steps: centralizing all civilian maritime forces and increasing their ability to accompany maritime traffic. Advocates of reliance on international law view this as a pathway for China to pursue its peaceful development strategy. The main reasoning behind this argument is that using military power to enforce law and order can have the unintended consequence of destabilizing the region and harming other economic development efforts. To avoid this catastrophe, they recommended that China use international law to the fullest extent and only use the PLAN as a deterrent force.[16]

Others have advocated for cooperating with regional partners to achieve maritime security. Several authors recommended that China work with the United States, Japan, India, and ASEAN states to establish trust among these nations. As it currently stands, other nations view any increase in China's naval spending as an act of aggression. The scholars hope that if China shows more transparency and cooperation, the world will be more accepting of a modern and powerful Chinese navy.[17]

Those who believed that China should go at it alone have adopted a more realist mentality and have very little faith in the international system. They argued that China should not leave its vital interest up to nations who do not necessarily share China's worldview. These scholars also argued that any type of international security cooperation efforts is likely to be U.S.-dominated and only used to enforce U.S. dominance of the world.

SCOPE OF CHINA'S NAVAL PRESENCE

New developments in international maritime law have made it necessary for China to expand the range of its naval capabilities. The question that many have asked, however, is how far should its power extend? As mentioned in chapter 1, UNCLOS, the current standard for maritime law, gives each nation an exclusive economic zone (EEZ) of up to 200 nautical miles from its coastline. Depending on how you demarcate China's territorial boundaries, this could be an enormous amount of area to govern. Additionally, because China is becoming a global power, some have argued that the PLAN should have global strike capabilities.

Some Chinese scholars developed a proposal that outlined the PLAN going through three phases of development over a fifty-year timeframe. The first phase would entail developing offshore operational capabilities that would include large-scale operational platforms and intermediate- and long-range precision guided weaponry. The second phase would include the addition of large and medium-size platforms capable of effectively controlling the offshore sea area up to its first island chain. In the third phase, the PLAN would transform into a regional navy that could operate in the Northwest Pacific and the open sea in its region. [18]

Evolution of the PLAN

The varying perspectives of authors, military personnel, and other influential individuals had an impact on the decision makers in China, resulting in a gradual shift in policy and the evolution of the nation's naval capabilities. This process has occurred over a period of nearly six decades and has resulted in China's greatly enhanced capabilities. The three phases of its development have been near-coast defense, near-sea active defense, and far-seas operations.

Near-Coast Defense Strategy

With coastlines that measure anywhere from the internationally recognized 14,500 kilometers to China's claimed 18,000-plus kilometers, the country had a challenge in simply securing its basic maritime boundaries. From the 1940s to the 1980s, the nation's policy essentially set out to protect the most strategic areas of the country, areas that any enemy could use to attack the mainland. The government identified three main locations as vital to the nation's security interest: the Straight of Bohai in the north—the maritime gateway to Tianjin and Beijing, the Straight of Taiwan in the east—the waterway between China and Taiwan, and the Strait of Quiongzhou in the south—an area that leads to strategic points in the southern part of the nation, for example, Hainan Island. China deployed a northern, eastern, and southern PLAN fleet to deal with the various threats to these areas. [19]

Sino–Soviet Rivalry

As the relationship between the Soviet Union and China became more and more adversarial, China began to view an invasion from the nation as one of its biggest security threats. Mao Zedong made the strategic decision to emphasize defending the nation against a possible Soviet attack from the north. China feared the Soviets would attempt to launch a two-pronged attack on land and sea using amphibious equipment. It believed these operations could lead to the capture of some of China's straits, islands, and other valuable assets.[20]

China ordered the PLAN to play an active role in the nation's defense against this threat. Its major responsibilities would be defending naval bases, harbors, and coastal airfields from attacks and also crippling Soviet supply ships to limit their ability to sustain a drawn-out ground campaign. During the 1950s and '60s, the Chinese government equipped the PLAN with weaponry to achieve these objectives. Its fleet was primarily composed of mine sweepers and torpedoes; gun and missile boats; light destroyers and frigates; and land-based, short-range naval bombers and Soviet-designed Romeo-class submarines.[21]

During the 1970s, however, the PLAN's weaponry began to slightly evolve. China started developing its first generation of Luda-class guided-missile destroyers and Jianghu-class guided-missile frigates. China also developed its first generation of Han-class nuclear-powered attack submarines. Also, later, it modified some of the ships to include surface-to-air missiles, helicopters, surveillance and fire-control radars, electronic warfare capabilities, CDSs, and higher-capacity surface-to-air missiles. China's nuclear submarine program allowed for the production of the weaponry. The government ended the program in 1962 and revived it in 1965 with the nationalistic aims of developing China's ability to build its own nuclear submarines.[22]

China accomplished its goal, but because the nation's technological knowledge was still in the development stage, it experienced major limitations to its naval fleet's capabilities. The most glaring down side was the limited range of attack capabilities. The surface-to-air missiles could only strike within eight to twelve kilometers and were unable to handle long-range airstrikes or sea-skimming antiship cruise missiles. China's naval equipment also had several other mechanical problems that limited its effectiveness far from the nation's coast, problems such as radiation leaks in submarines, an inability to launch missiles while submerged, and various reliability concerns. These shortcomings inspired China to continue to create new technologies and eventually to totally revamp its naval strategy.[23]

First and Second Taiwan Strait Crisis

Despite the fact that the Soviet Union was such a dominant and powerful foe, some scholars argued that the nation that created the biggest concern for China was Taiwan. Many within China held the belief that the KMT government would stage a sea-based attack in an effort to recapture the mainland. This threat caused China to not only develop self-defense mechanisms but to also stage some offensives against Taiwan. These skirmishes drew international attention and led to a few direct standoffs between the PLAN and international naval forces.

In addition, the outbreak of the Korean War in 1950 put the United States right in the heart of the battle between Taiwan and China. For years, the United States had chosen to remain neutral in the various battles between differing factions in China, but because the United States had many troops near the area, it changed its policy. Also, America's Cold War efforts to prevent the further spread of communism made the protection of Taiwan a crucial part of its strategy. The Truman administration declared the straits neutral waters and decided to send a naval vessel to the area to ensure that neither side attacked each other.[24]

When President Eisenhower took office and the Korean War came to an end, he also lifted the naval blockade. China and Taiwan saw this policy change as an opportunity to reposition themselves for a possible standoff, so Taiwan's leader, Chiang Kai-Shek, moved 58,000 troops to Quemoy and 15,000 to Matsu in 1954. This move sparked anger within mainland China and led the Chinese government to make a declaration to "liberate" Taiwan. The United States attempted to persuade China against attacking Taiwan, but without a strong naval presence in the area, it was unable to enforce its wishes. In September of the same year, China began bombing islands, sparking U.S. outrage and calls for action. Some proposed using nuclear warfare to neutralize China. President Eisenhower refused to take this approach and instead opted to sign a mutual defense treaty with the government of Taiwan in 1954. The agreement, formally named the U.S.–Republic of China Mutual Defense Treaty, essentially guaranteed that the United States would defend Taiwan in the case of an attack from China.[25]

China attempted to circumvent this treaty by attacking islands claimed by Taiwan. This strategy put the United States in a precarious position because it did not know whether the areas fell within the territory it agreed to protect. The Formosa Resolution, which passed both houses of congress in January 1955, clarified the issue. The resolution committed the United States to the defense of Taiwan and gave the president the authorization to rapidly deploy troops to prevent an eminent attack. The resolution also clarified the areas off of mainland Taiwan that would be included in this protection.[26] Also, the United States would not remove a nuclear attack as an option during the negotiations. This stance drew condemnation from the international community, but this hard-line approach ultimately forced China to cease its hostilities and begin negotiating with Taiwan. In 1955, China ended its military offensives on the islands, effectively, and temporarily, ending the crisis.[27]

In 1958, China began bombing the Quemoy and Matsu Islands again. Taiwan viewed these attacks as an attempt by Mao to assert his independence from the Soviet Union. The United States again stood strongly behind Taiwan, forcing China to negotiate rather than enter into a direct military confrontation with the United States. This second crisis came to an end in October 1958 when Chinese Defense Minister Marshall Peng Dehuai offered to negotiate a peace settlement. The United States' strong support for Taiwan had twice averted a major crisis, but it did not permanently change China's stance. As China moved further and further away from the Soviet Union and eventually normalized relations with the United States, the diplomatic balance of power in the region became much more complex. [28]

EXPANSION UNDER DENG XIAOPING

Following the death of Mao Zedong, Deng Xiaoping took control of China and moved the country's naval strategy in a different direction. The policy he implemented called for a robust expansion of China's naval capabilities, with the aim of extending its reach to at least two hundred nautical miles. The new operational distance it hoped to achieve extended to what China defines as the Second Island Chain, which is located east of Japan and ends slightly before the U.S. territory of Guam. The main objectives of this new policy was to reunify Taiwan with the mainland, restore lost and disputed territories, protect China's maritime resources, secure sea lines of communication during times of war, deter and defend against sea-based foreign aggression, and achieve strategic nuclear deterrence. [29]

In 1995, China had another military confrontation with Taiwan. The spark to the hostilities came after Taiwanese president Lee Teng-hui went to the United States. His trip ended a long period of international isolation in Taiwan and portrayed Taiwan as an independent nation. This portrayal angered the Chinese officials, who had been actively pursuing its one-China policy, and in response, they launched a series of missile tests near Taiwan. These tests drew strong international condemnation, and they failed to damage the legitimacy of the Taiwanese government. Presidential elections proceeded as scheduled in 1996, and Lee Teng-hui became the nation's first popularly elected president. [30]

Modernization of Naval Equipment

Beginning in the 1990s, the PLAN began to improve its forces around four core elements: frigates and destroyers, submarines, naval fighters, and antiship missiles. These advancements were inspired by the lessons learned from its previous naval encounters. After the nation became more aware of the needs for a strong navy and the economy grew to the point to enable the financing of research and development, China began to see rapid advances in its capabilities. From 2002 to 2004, China successfully launched thirteen new submarines, and in 2003 alone, it initiated construction on more than seventy military ships.[31]

This increase in capacity has given China the ability to move ten thousand troops into a war zone. By 2009, researchers estimated that China possessed seventy-two modern frigates and destroyers, fifty-eight submarines, fifty medium and heavy amphibious ships, and forty-one missile patrol boats. By 2011, the PLAN possessed seventy-five surface combatants, more than sixty submarines, fifty-five medium and large amphibious ships, and approximately eighty-five missile-equipped small combatants. Also in 2011, the PLAN completed the construction of a significant naval base at Yulin, located on the southernmost tip of Hainan Island. The base is large enough to house a combination of attack and ballistic missile submarines and sophisticated surface combatants, including aircraft carriers. Submarine tunnel facilities at the base could also potentially enable deployments from the facility with reduced risk of discovery.[32]

Far-Seas Capability

Many have wondered what China would chose to do with its newly found naval power. Some view it as a major threat, while others see China as another possible collaborator in the efforts to ensure safe global shipping lanes. In 2008, China became a major player in the securing of the waters off the coast of Somalia. The deployment was the PLAN's first mission outside of Chinese territorial waters and the first time a Chinese warship had visited Africa since the extensive trade between imperial China and East African empires began to taper off in the fifteenth century. China also had its first-ever naval exercise in the Mediterranean Sea in February 2011, when it rescued thirty thousand of its citizens from Libya during its civil war.[33]

Another first for China's naval forces came in March 2011 when it provided an escort for the World Food Program (WFP) ship *Amina*. China's *Ma'anshan* escorted *Amina* from the port of Berbera in the Somaliland region to the port of Bossaso in the Puntland region of Somalia. *Ma'anshan* is capable of carrying cruise and surface-to-air missiles and also contains a helicopter. Special forces fighters man the boat, giving it full attack capabilities for when it needs it. China decided to volunteer to escort the WFP ship after it received the message that the EU had called for additional nations to help patrol the region to ensure the safe delivery of aid to the populations decimated by the persistent drought of 2011.[34] China has also agreed to collaborate with other nations patrolling the region by becoming a part of a maritime initiative named Shared Awareness and Deconfliction (Shade), an organization that protects segments of the Western Indian Ocean. Two additional Chinese ships, the *Xuzhou* and the *Khoushan,* have been making port calls to various countries along the East African coast in an effort to foster positive relations.

Some nations, particularly those in the disputed South China Sea region, are concerned about China's massive buildup of naval capabilities.[35] They believe that the experience China is gaining from fighting against the piracy in the Gulf of Aden and the Indian Ocean will embolden it to take more aggressive measures so it can gain control of these aforementioned disputed areas. The United States and the EU, however, welcome China's participation in the international efforts to patrol the massive region impacted by Somali piracy. China's defense ministry has proclaimed that its naval forces have rescued nine ships that Somali pirates hijacked and prevented the hijacking of thirty-three others in the Gulf of Aden. Because China ships billions of dollars of goods to Africa and the massive investment it continues to make on the continent, it is almost certain that China will continue to use all the options at its disposal to help eradicate piracy and ensure the safe passage of vessels.[36]

Aspirations for Regional Dominance

After years of a primarily land-based military force with very limited maritime capability, China has made dramatic strides. The PLAN now contains Asia's largest collection of principle combatants, submarines, and amphibious warships and is fully able to project itself in the far seas as demonstrated by its involvement in Somalia and Libya. The question that remains to be answered is whether China will use its increased capability to dominate the region and enforce its claims in the SCS.[37]

Since China is the undisputed giant of the region, many have looked to the United States to counter its influence. As mentioned earlier in the chapter, the United States has gotten involved in the region on several occasions, but in general, it has simply encouraged the peaceful resolution of various conflicts. The following chapter outlines in detail the interest of the United States in the region and how those interests have evolved over the past several decades.

NOTES

1. "The Dragon's New Teeth: A Rare Look inside the World's Biggest Military Expansion," *The Economist,* April 17, 2012, [online] http://www.economist.com/node/21552193. Accessed November 3, 2012.

2. Central Intelligence Agency, "China," *World Factbook,* 2013, [online] https://www.cia.gov/library/publications/the-world-factbook/geos/ch.html. Accessed March 31, 2013.

3. Benjamin Armstrong, "China . . . from the Sea: The Importance of Chinese Naval History," *Strategic Insights,* vol. 6, no. 7, December 2007, [online] http://www.dtic.mil/cgi-bin/GetTRDoc?AD=ADA519989. Accessed April 12, 2013.

4. Ibid.

5. Ibid.

6. Ibid.
7. Ibid.
8. Ibid.
9. Donald S. Zageria, *Breaking the China–Taiwan Impasse* (Westport, CT: Praeger, 2003).
10. Daniel M. Hartnett and Frederic Vellucci, "Towards a Maritime Strategy: An Analysis of Chinese Views since the Early 1990's," in Phillip C. Saunders, Christopher D. Yung, Michael Swaine, and Andrew Nein-Dzu Yang ed., *The Chinese Navy: Expanding Capabilities, Evolving Roles* (Washington, DC: National Defense University Press, 2011), pp. 81–82.
11. Ibid., pp. 83–84.
12. Ibid., pp. 88–91.
13. Ibid., pp. 92–94.
14. Ibid.
15. Ibid., pp. 95–97.
16. Ibid.
17. Ibid.
18. Ibid., pp. 98–102.
19. Nan Li, "The Evolution of China's Naval Strategy and Capabilities: From 'Near Coast' and 'Near Seas' to 'Far Seas,'" in Phillip C. Saunders, Christopher D. Yung, Michael Swaine, and Andrew Nein-Dzu Yang ed., *The Chinese Navy: Expanding Capabilities, Evolving Roles* (Washington, DC: National Defense University Press, 2011), pp. 111–16.
20. "A Country Study: China," *Library of Congress Country Studies*, August 24, 2012, [online] http://lcweb2.loc.gov/frd/cs/cntoc.html. Accessed, March 24, 2013.
21. Li, pp. 111–16.
22. Ibid.
23. Ibid.
24. "Korean War," *History*, 2013, [online] http://www.history.com/topics/korean-war. Accessed April 12, 2012.
25. Li, pp. 111–16.
26. Andrew Glass, "House Approves Formosa Resolution, Jan. 25, 1955," *Politico*, January 25, 2011, [online] http://www.politico.com/news/stories/0111/48058.html. Accessed April 12, 2013.
27. "Milestones: 1953–1960," *U.S. Department of State, Office of the Historian*, n.d., [online] http://history.state.gov/milestones/1953-1960/TaiwanSTraitCrises. Accessed April 12, 2013.
28. Ibid.
29. Li, pp. 116–25.
30. "Taiwan Strait: 21 July 1995 to 23 March 1996," *GlobalSecurity.org*, 2013, [online] http://www.globalsecurity.org/military/ops/taiwan_strait.htm. Accessed April 12, 2013.
31. Christian Bedford, "The View from the West: Chinese Naval Power in the 21st Century," *Canadian Naval Review*, Summer 2009, vol. 5, no. 2, pp. 34–35, [online] http://www.navalreview.ca/wp-content/uploads/public/vol5num2/vol5num2art8.pdf. Accessed April 9, 2012.
32. "Annual Report to Congress: Military and Security Developments Involving the People's Republic of China 2011," *Department of Defense*, May 6, 2012, [online] http://www.defense.gov/pubs/pdfs/2011_CMPR_Final.pdf. Accessed November 5, 2012.
33. Christopher L. Daniels, *Somali Piracy and Terrorism in the Horn of Africa* (Lanham, MD: Scarecrow Press, 2012), pp. 73–74; "Chinese Navy Sails Another First off Somalia," *Wall Street Journal*, March 30, 2011.
34. Ibid.
35. Daniels, pp. 73–74; "China's Anti-Piracy Role off Somalia Expands," *BBC News*, January 29, 2010.
36. "China's Anti-Piracy Role."

37. "Dragon's New Teeth"; "Annual Report to Congress."

FIVE

U.S. Involvement and Interest in the South China Sea

The United States has had extensive interest in the Asian region for the last century. Several major wars have been fought within the territory, leading to the loss of hundreds of thousands of American lives and dramatically impacting U.S. foreign policy. This chapter outlines some of the major conflicts that the United States has been involved with in the Asian Pacific region during the last century and gives an analysis of the nation's current political and economic interest in the region.

THE U.S.–PHILIPPINE WAR

At the turn of the twentieth century, the United States found itself embroiled in a war in its territory in the Philippines. The Philippines had previously been a Spanish colony for more than three hundred years, and in the early 1890s, it began a major rebellion to end colonial rule. The United States provided support to the Filipino nationalists, leading to their victory over the Spaniards and the declaration of the First Filipino Republic. This victory was short lived, however, because of the U.S. victory over the Spanish in the Spanish–American War.[1]

Following the end of the hostilities between the United States and Spain, Spain ceded the Philippines and Guam to the United States. The U.S. populace argued over what it should do with the territory. Some advocated maintaining control of the area to further U.S. economic interest in the region, while others' main goal was to ensure that rival nations, such as Germany and Japan, would not gain control of the territory. Some wanted to remain in control of the area because of their belief that the Filipinos were incapable of self-rule and Filipino governance could ultimately destabilize the region.[2]

On the other hand, several individuals argued that the United States should avoid getting involved in colonial activities in the Philippines. The strongest arguments came from those who took the position that it was against the moral values of the United States to colonize another nation. With the exception of its role in Liberia, the United States had avoided getting involved in colonialism in Africa, and many preferred it take the same approach in Asia. Many also believed bringing the Philippines in as a U.S. territory would eventually open the door for representatives of Filipino descent to serve in the U.S. government. Those who opposed the United States taking control of the area waged many other arguments, but ultimately, the United States did colonize the area, and this move sparked outrage among the Filipino population.[3]

Revolutionaries led by Emilio Aguinaldo seized control of most of the Philippines' main island of Luzon and proclaimed the area the independent Philippine Republic. The United States refused to accept the Filipinos' demands for freedom and took decisive measures to assert its sovereignty over the area. This brought the United States in direct confrontation with soldiers claiming to represent the Philippine Republic, leading to several deadly standoffs.[4]

By 1899, these periodic standoffs had grown into an all-out bloody war. The U.S. government attempted to refer to the conflict as a mere insurrection to prevent people from perceiving it as a war of aggression. Despite these efforts, the war still became very unpopular among the American people, who were largely in favor of focusing on the western hemisphere instead of pursuing expansionist policies in Asia. Several newspapers ran articles criticizing U.S. action, but the conflict still lasted for years.[5]

For the first nine months, the war was mainly a conventional engagement pitting the Philippine troops against American military personnel. Fighting in this manner put the Philippines at a strong disadvantage, leading to disastrous outcomes. The United States had a strong advantage in the conflict because it had formally trained soldiers, a consistent supply of modern weaponry, and superior naval capabilities, which allowed it to easily blockade the island. The Filipino fighters, on the other hand, had little to no outside support for their cause, limited access to weapons and ammunition, and a host of other logistical issues. As a result of this imbalance of power, thousands of Philippine soldiers died.[6]

The large amounts of casualties suffered caused the Philippine troops to convert to guerrilla warfare. Although this shift in tactic favored the Philippine soldiers, it ultimately led to horrific atrocities committed against its citizenry. Filipinos have detailed accounts where they accuse American soldiers of using brutal tactics and unnecessarily and indiscriminately killing Philippine nationals. Also, the United States accused

Philippine soldiers of brutalizing Americans taken captive and mutilating the dead bodies of U.S. soldiers. Thousands of others died from various diseases, such as malaria and cholera, and also from the food shortages caused by the protracted warfare.[7]

The combination of the continuous fighting, large amount of U.S. troop involvement, escalating casualties, and domestic pressure made the United States consider taking a different strategy to end the uprising. President Truman attempted to divide the Philippine people by negotiating with elites who did not agree with Aguinaldo's plan for the future of the nation. The program also granted a degree of political autonomy and introduced social reforms and plans for economic development. Over time, this approach gained in popularity, and by 1902, the war had ended.[8]

There were several other rebellions that periodically occurred in the nation, showing that parts of the population still desired independence. Despite these uprisings, the United States remained in control of the territory until 1946, when it granted the nation its independence.

GUAM

The United States acquired Guam following its victory in the Spanish–American War. In 1899, President William McKinley issued an executive order placing Guam under the control of the navy. The island's first appointed governor was Captain R. P. Leary, who made several changes to the administration. These adjustments helped to modernize the country and stimulate economic growth. In 1941, Japanese forces attacked and captured Guam. During its occupation of Guam, Japanese soldiers brutalized the citizenry, making them long for liberation. By 1944, the United States was able to defeat Japan and reclaim control of the island. The United States immediately converted several parts of the island into forward-operating bases in order to prepare for any future conflicts in the region. In 1950, the United States passed the Guam Organic Act, which made the nation an unincorporated territory of the United States. The act also created the first indigenously controlled government on the island.[9]

The population of the island has grown to more than 160,000, and its economy is still primarily driven by tourism and U.S. defense spending. The island is home to Andersen Air Force Base and is still one of the United States' most significant military outposts.[10] (More details about its current operations are given later in the chapter.)

PEARL HARBOR

Prior to 9/11, Pearl Harbor was one of the deadliest and most memorable attacks on U.S. soil by a foreign entity. This attack exposed weaknesses in the U.S. military's defense systems and demonstrated that Asian nations were powerful enough to strike the United States. The United States and Japan were developing an ever-increasing adversarial relationship due to continued Japanese aggression toward China. The Japanese saw China as an ideal territory for expansion in order to fuel its rapid demographic growth. In 1937, Japan declared war on China, and the United States responded by placing sanctions and embargoes on the nation, aimed at curbing its imperialistic ways. Unfortunately, the United States did not reach its desired outcome; in fact, the sanctions made relations between the United States and Japan deteriorate even further. Negotiations consistently ended in stalemates, making the prospect of war between the nations a more likely reality.[11]

The only question was, Where would a standoff between the United States and Japan take place? People assumed the conflict would take place in an area in Asia that the United States or one of its allies controlled but certainly not on the Hawaiian islands. Pearl Harbor was home to nearly the entire Pacific fleet and airfields with hundreds of military aircraft. The military was not heavily defending the area because the United States did not believe that an attack would occur there. The combination of the significant number of high-value targets and the limited defense mechanisms in place made an attack irresistible for Japan.[12]

In planning the attack, Japan's strategic goal was to destroy America's Pacific fleet and make the nation unable to retaliate. Japan had strong aspirations of dominating the resource-rich nations in southeast Asia and was aware that the United States was the only major power in its way. The United States, on the other hand, had growing interest in the region because of its presence in the Philippines and Guam and its economic investments in several other nations in the area. The nations' opposing goals put them in direct conflict with each other on a continual basis, and Japan sought to put an end to the conflict.

On the morning of December 7, 1941, hundreds of Japanese airplanes headed to Pearl Harbor to launch the surprise attack. The first vessel that was destroyed was the battleship USS *Arizona*. The Japanese bombs pounded the ship and caused it to sink. More than a thousand men aboard were killed by the surprise attack. Also, a number of torpedoes hit the USS *Oklahoma*, which capsized, and more than 400 members of its crew perished.[13]

By the time the attack ended, every battleship in Pearl Harbor—USS *Arizona*, USS *Oklahoma*, USS *California*, USS *West Virginia*, USS *Utah*, USS *Maryland*, USS *Pennsylvania*, USS *Tennessee*, and USS *Nevada*—was severely damaged. In sum, the Japanese attack on Pearl Harbor crippled or destroyed eighteen American ships and nearly three hundred airplanes. Most significantly, 2,500 men were killed and another 1,000 were wounded, making this one of the deadliest events in U.S. history.[14]

Even though the attack on Pearl Harbor was a horrific incident, it failed to achieve its objective of eliminating the United States' ability to strike in the Pacific. The military rebuilt most of the damaged ships, but more importantly, the most strategic aircraft carriers were mostly undamaged. Also, another positive for the United States was that the base's onshore infrastructure was mainly left in place. The oil storage facilities, repair shops, shipyards, and submarine docks were all still functional following the attack.

Policy Shift

The biggest long-term impact of the attack on Pearl Harbor is the way it changed American foreign policy. Before the attack, the majority of the population proscribed to an isolationist mind-set and was firmly against U.S. intervention in overseas conflicts. After the attack, however, the majority of the American people were united in their determination to go to war. This event showed that no matter how far away the enemy may be, with modern technology, they have the capability to launch an attack on your mainland. It also demonstrated the strategic significance of the Asian region and caused the United States to focus more of its attention there. On December 8, 1941, President Roosevelt declared war on Japan, and days later, Germany and Italy declared war on the United States. This drew the United States into World War II on both the European and Pacific fronts.

PACIFIC FRONT OF WORLD WAR II

The Philippines

In 1941, the U.S. Department of War established a new command to organize the defense of the Philippines. General Douglas MacArthur ran the command named the U.S. Armed Forces, Far East. Tensions had been steadily rising between the United States and the Japanese, and this command was established to protect American interest. It was composed of a combination of Philippine and American troops that teamed up to protect the island. The command was still in its development stages when it received its first major challenge from the Japanese.[15]

Just ten hours after its brutal attack on Pearl Harbor, the Japanese launched a surprise attack on the Philippines. Japan strategically planned for the attack to occur at a time when the United States could not quickly send reinforcements to support its position. By January 1942, the Japanese were able to cripple the United States' aerial and naval forces and occupy the capital city of Manila. The United States continued to resist, but by May of the same year, General Wainwright, who took over the command after MacArthur was forced to flee to Australia, surrendered, causing the beginning of a period of Japanese occupation of the island.[16]

During its rule of the nation, Japan brutalized prisoners of war and enforced its authority using a combination of harsh tactics and appeasement of elites. Initially, the Japanese played on the Filipino people's strong desire to gain its independence. After governing through the Council of State for over a year, the Japanese declared the Philippines an independent republic in October 1943. The composition of the government mainly consisted of the Philippine elite who desired to alleviate the harsh rule of the Japanese and protect their own interest. Some within the government were also informants for the United States and assisted in its efforts to retake the island.[17]

Also, hundreds of thousands of Filipinos who belonged to guerrilla organizations opposed the Japanese occupation. These guerrillas limited the extent of Japanese rule and proved to be a major impediment to it establishing a long-standing presence in the country. The United States provided support to these rebel forces, and eventually a consensus was developed that the two sides would collaborate to end Japanese rule.[18]

In October 1944, America began its campaign to regain control of the Philippines. The first portion of the campaign began on the island of Leyte. Japanese forces were sparsely located in the area, so the United States regained control of the territory with very little resistance. The Japanese made the strategic calculation to station the majority of its forces on Luzon, and this tactic drew the United States into one of its biggest campaigns in the Pacific theater of the war. The fighting was exceptionally brutal in the mountainous areas of Luzon, where the Japanese stationed thousands of troops. Even as it became apparent that America would retake the island, Japanese soldiers continued to fight to the end. Despite this persistence, the United States forced Japan to surrender. In total, the Japanese lost more than 300,000 troops, and the United States lost 14,000 in this bloody battle. On the Filipino side, some have estimated that as many as one million citizens were killed. In addition, the battles caused extensive damage to major cities, specifically to the country's infrastructure.[19]

Following the conclusion of the hostilities, the Philippines gained its long-awaited independence in 1946. The United States maintained several military installations in the country until several of the lease agreements expired. In 2012, however, the United States engaged in talks about reestablishing some U.S. military installations in the region.

Guam

The Japanese also attacked the Island of Guam immediately following its bombardment of Pearl Harbor. Within four days, the Japanese gained control of the island, sparking another military standoff with the United

States. The United States planned to use all of the necessary resources to regain control of the island because it held one of the most strategic locations in the region.[20]

The U.S. naval forces and its allied partners had slowly begun to regroup after the initial shock caused by Japan's aggression. They launched the successful Guadalcanal campaign, which resulted in the recapturing of some of the territories claimed by Japan, such as Saipan. The forces' next major focus was to reclaim Guam, which would prove to be a major challenge.[21]

The biggest concern of Guam's citizens was that the military forces on the island would damage the physical environment. Guam is full of coral reefs, rugged cliffs, and other challenging terrain. The United States deployed the Third Marine Division and the Army Seventy-Seventh Infantry Division to take on the challenge of reclaiming the island. The battle commenced in July 1944 on two different fronts. The Third Marine Division landed near Agana to the north of Orote, and the First Provisional Marine Brigade landed near Agat to the south.[22]

They met strong resistance from Japanese personnel but would ultimately successfully enter the shore. Once on the land, the two sides battled it out over a seventeen-day period. The American forces would emerge victorious and reclaim sovereignty over the island. Japan lost more than 18,000 soldiers in the battle, while the United States only lost 1,400. One of Japan's most significant naval commanders, Takashina Takeshi, was also killed in the battle, further hampering the nation's capabilities. This battle marked a turning point and demonstrated that the United States was capable of defeating Japan in its own region.[23]

As discussed earlier in the chapter, Guam remains an extremely strategic location for the United States and is home to large numbers of military personnel. The command centers there are heavily involved in the United States' response to any conflict within the Asia-Pacific realm.

BOMBING AND OCCUPATION OF JAPAN

Although Japan suffered several defeats, it refused to surrender to the American forces. By 1945, the United States had already defeated the German forces in Europe, and Japan only had a slim chance of winning the war. Despite these odds, Japan remained insistent on continuing its fight and was successful in causing the casualties of thousands of U.S. servicemen. The Allies offered Japan one final chance to cease hostilities through the Potsdam Declaration. The document delivered an ultimatum to Japan to either surrender or face "prompt and utter destruction." Japan's refusal of the offer and the seemingly endless warfare between the United States and Japan motivated some to think that the United States should employ a more efficient method of ending the war.[24]

MacArthur and other top military officials favored continuing the use of conventional warfare and following up with a large-scale invasion of the Japanese mainland, which was given the code name "Operation Downfall." Although they were confident that the United States would emerge victorious, they also understood that the cost of the war would be high. Military advisers estimated that more than one million U.S. troops could be lost in such an invasion. This led President Eisenhower to consider using an atomic weapon despite the disapproval he received from several members of his cabinet.[25]

The process of developing a nuclear weapon ensued in 1942 under the name "Manhattan Project." The U.S. Army Corps of Engineers spearheaded the construction of the facilities needed for the top-secret program, and over the next several years, teams of scientists from the United States and other Allied nations worked on producing the key materials that would be used in the bomb. Once they produced the uranium and plutonium, they were sent to the labs in Los Alamos, New Mexico, where Robert J. Oppenheimer's team worked to turn these raw materials into a nuclear weapon. The program was very effective, resulting in the successful test of a plutonium bomb in Alamogordo, New Mexico, in July 1945.[26]

Faced with two options, a drawn-out expensive war that could cost up to a million American lives or quick decisive victory, Truman decided to order the bombing of Japan. The first target the U.S. government chose was Hiroshima, a town of roughly 350,000 outside of Tokyo. The B-29 bomber *Enola Gay* dropped the nine-thousand-pound uranium bomb named "Little Boy" on August 6, 1945. The massive explosion destroyed five square miles of the city and left the Japanese people in awe. Even after this shocking event, Japan did not surrender, and the United States moved to drop another bomb on the nation. On August 9, 1945, the United States dropped a ten-thousand-pound plutonium bomb named "Fat Man" on the city of Nagasaki. The bomb also inflicted unimaginable amounts of damage and finally broke the will of the Japanese government. On noon of the same day, Emperor Hirohito announced Japan's surrender and signed a formal agreement with the United States on September 2, 1945.[27]

Occupation of Japan

To ensure another outbreak of hostilities would not occur, the United States occupied Japan following its victory over the nation. Japan had to dismantle its military and establish other political and economic reforms. As a result, Japanese society underwent a dramatic change, but other nations were concerned that without economic growth, Japan would eventually fall to the rising wave of communism creeping through the region. Therefore, the United States established several military bases across the country, many of which still exist today, and signed a security assistance pact that essentially guaranteed the nation's defense.[28]

As the hostilities from the Second World War began to dwindle, a threat from the east began to rise. The fight against the spread of communism again sent U.S. forces to the Asian region, this time on the Korean peninsula.

KOREAN CONFLICT

In 1950, North Korea drew the United States into battle on the Korean peninsula after it invaded South Korea. The two sides had a history of battling each other, but the Cold War dynamics made the peninsula's internal battles an international conflict. The anticommunist dictator Syngman Rhee controlled the south, and the United States supported him. On the other hand, communist dictator Kim Il Sung governed the north, and the Soviet Union supported him. These factors made this battle one of the first major military showdowns in the Cold War era and a test of the newly formulated U.S. policy of containment.[29]

The war began as primarily a defense effort aimed at removing communists from South Korea. This strategy went badly because North Korea's forces were more disciplined and capable than the South Korean soldiers. Also, climatic and hygienic issues caused trouble for U.S. forces. Those difficulties motivated the United States to switch to a more offensive strategy aimed at weakening the communists in the north. Initially, the new strategy was a success. An amphibious assault at Inchon pushed the North Koreans out of Seoul and back to their side of the thirty-eighth parallel. However, once American troops crossed the boundary and headed north toward the Yalu River, the border between North Korea and communist China, the Chinese started to worry about protecting themselves from what they called "armed aggression against Chinese territory."[30]

China felt motivated to intervene in the conflict, causing a frustrating stalemate that tested U.S. strategy. Some within America wanted to continue fighting until South Korea reached a decisive victory, while others, such as Truman, wanted to end the conflict as soon as possible and avoid a bigger conflict with China or the Soviet Union. Truman and MacArthur held oppositional views; as a result, Truman fired MacArthur for insubordination. After two years of negotiations, North Korea and South Korea signed a peace agreement on July 27, 1953. This agreement gave South Korea an additional 1,500 square miles beyond the traditional thirty-eighth parallel and allowed POWs to remain where they chose. The agreement also created the two-mile demilitarized zone, which is still recognized to this day.[31]

The war cost five million people their lives in total. Forty thousand Americans were killed and an additional 100,000 were wounded in the battle. Today, the United States maintains a military presence in South Korea, with thousands of troops stationed in the country.[32]

VIETNAM WAR

The war in Vietnam is one of the most well-documented and controversial conflicts in U.S. history. After the Northern Vietnamese forces defeated the French colonial administration, they made moves to unite the country under one communist banner. Unlike the North, the government in the South desired a Vietnam with a close alliance with western nations. This difference put the two sides in direct conflict with each other. The United States had provided advisers and trainers to help support the southern government, but it soon realized it needed a stronger show of force. In 1965, the United States introduced active combat units into the country, and by 1969, the U.S. government stationed more than 500,000 U.S. military personnel in Vietnam.[33]

To combat the U.S. influence, the Soviet Union and the Chinese government poured millions of dollars' worth of weapons, supplies, and military trainers into North Vietnam. The intervention of these external forces proved to be a major challenge for the United States. As the war dragged on and became more and more expensive, it lost the popular support of the American public. U.S. forces withdrew from the country in 1973, and by 1975, South Vietnam was overrun by a full-scale invasion by the North Vietnamese. The war proved to be very deadly, claiming the lives of more than two million Vietnamese. In addition, the United States lost nearly 58,000 troops in the conflict.[34]

The Vietnam War was the last large-scale military conflict the United States would get involved in in the Asian Pacific region. Over time, U.S. interest shifted from the singular goal of containment of communism to engagement and the eventual capitalizing of the enormous economic opportunities that exist in the region.

REESTABLISHMENT OF RELATIONS WITH CHINA

The United States ended its diplomatic relations with China after its communist revolution in 1949. For two solid decades, the relationship between China and the United States was extremely adversarial, resulting in several indirect military standoffs. As ties between China and the Soviet Union began to deteriorate, officials within the U.S. government saw an opportunity to engage and use China as a hedge against Soviet expansion. President Richard Nixon made a bold visit to China in 1972, breaking the years of silence between the two nations and marking a new chapter in American foreign policy. Nixon had a strong history of opposition to communism; his stance gave him the political leverage to negotiate with China without causing much uproar within the American political community.[35]

The planning for the visit began when Henry Kissinger made a secret trip to China in 1971 and a subsequent follow-up meeting later on in the same year. These preliminary visits set the stage for Nixon's monumental meeting with Mao Zedong in 1972. During this meeting, the two sides agreed on several key issues, but Taiwan continued to be a major sticking point. This disagreement caused the full normalization of diplomatic relations between the United States and China to be delayed until 1979, when President Jimmy Carter took office.[36]

The normalization of U.S.–China relations helped to pave the way for China to become a willing participant in the international community. It also encouraged China to liberalize its economy and allow foreign investments in the nation.

AMERICAN INTEREST IN ASIA

As mentioned in chapter 3, several American companies have moved their operations to Asia in an attempt to maximize their profit margins. Every year, the United States imports billions of goods and services from the region, and this number is continually growing. Several American energy companies have a vested interest in the region as a potential source to increase their global presence. These developments have caused the Obama administration to focus its attention on Asia and the conflict in the South China Sea.

In the beginning of President Obama's second term as president, he announced his administration's intentions to "pivot" its focus from the Middle East to Asia. He also specified that the United States would not simply focus in on Northeast Asia as the nation has done in the past but would also engage with Southeast Asian nations as well. This move places the United States directly in the heart of the SCS debate. To date, the United States has refrained from taking sides and has instead simply advocated for a peaceful resolution of the debate.[37]

U.S. interest in Asia has evolved dramatically over the course of the last century, and the evidence now shows that both regional and international efforts will need to be initiated to bring a resolution to this dispute. The concluding chapter examines the global significance of the SCS conflict and offers policy recommendations to bring about its resolution.

NOTES

1. "The Philippine–American War, 1899–1902," *U.S. Department of State, Office of the Historian*, n.d., [online] http://history.state.gov/milestones/1899-1913/War. Accessed April 13, 2013.

2. Ibid.

3. Ibid.

4. Ibid.

5. "The Philippine War: A Conflict of Conscience for African Americans," *National Park Service*, 2013, [online] http://www.nps.gov/prsf/historyculture/the-philippine-insurrectiothe-philippine-war-a-conflict-of-consciencen-a-war-of-controversy.htm. Accessed April 13, 2013.

6. Luzviminda Francisco, "The First Vietnam: U.S.–Philippine War of 1899," *History Is a Weapon*, 1973, [online] http://historyisaweapon.com/defcon1/franciscofirstvietnam.html. Accessed April 10, 2013; E. San Juan Jr., "U.S. Genocide in the Philippines: A Case of Guilt, Shame, or Amnesia?" *Selves and Others*, March 22, 2005, [online] http://web.archive.org/web/20080430182246/http://www.selvesandothers.org/article9315.html. Accessed April 5, 2013.

7. Ibid.

8. "Philippine–American War, 1899–1902."

9. "History," *Naval Base Guam*, n.d., [online] http://www.cnic.navy.mil/regions/jrm/installations/navbase_guam/about/history.html. Accessed April 12, 2013.

10. Central Intelligence Agency, "Guam," *World Factbook*, 2013, [online] https://www.cia.gov/library/publications/the-world-factbook/geos/gq.html. Accessed, March 29, 2013.

11. "Pearl Harbor," *History*, 2013, [online] http://www.history.com/topics/pearl-harbor. Accessed June 5, 2013.

12. Ibid.

13. Ibid.

14. Ibid.

15. "U.S. Army Campaigns: WWII—Asiatic-Pacific Theater," *U.S. Army Center of Military History*, November 19, 2010, [online] http://www.history.army.mil/html/reference/army_flag/ww2_ap.html. Accessed April 10, 2013.

16. Ibid.

17. Ibid.

18. "Philippines: World War II, 1941–45," *Library of Congress Country Studies*, June 1991, [online] http://lcweb2.loc.gov/cgi-bin/query/r?frd/cstdy:@field(DOCID+ph0033). Accessed March 24, 2013.

19. Ibid.

20. David Lotz and Rose S. N. Manibusan, "Liberation—Guam Remembers," *National Park Service*, n.d., [online] http://www.nps.gov/history/history/online_books/npswapa/extContent/Lib/liberation16.htm. Accessed April 15, 2013.

21. "Guadalcanal Campaign, August 1942–February 1943, Overview and Special Image Selection," *Naval History and Heritage Command*, n.d., [online] http://www.history.navy.mil/photos/events/wwii-pac/guadlcnl/guadlcnl.htm. Accessed April 15, 2013.

22. Lotz and Manibusan.

23. Ibid.

24. "The Bombing of Hiroshima and Nagasaki," *History*, 2013, [online] http://www.history.com/topics/bombing-of-hiroshima-and-nagasaki. Accessed April 15, 2013.

25. "Japan: World War II and the Occupation, 1941–52," *Library of Congress Country Studies*, January 1994, [online]http://lcweb2.loc.gov/cgi-bin/query/r?frd/cstdy:@field(DOCID+jp0046). Accessed, March 24, 2013.

26. "Bombing of Hiroshima and Nagasaki."

27. Ibid.

28. "Milestones: 1945–1952," *U.S. Department of State, Office of the Historian,* n.d., [online] http://history.state.gov/milestones/1945-1952/JapanReconstruction. Accessed April 15, 2013.

29. "The Korean War, June 1950–July 1953," *Naval Heritage and History Command,* n.d., [online] http://www.history.navy.mil/photos/events/kowar/kowar.htm. Accessed April 12, 2013.

30. Ibid.; "South Korea: The Korean War, 1950–53," *Library of Congress Country Studies,* June 1990, [online] http://lcweb2.loc.gov/cgi-bin/query/r?frd/cstdy:@field(DOCID+kr0026). Accessed March 24, 2013.

31. "Korean War," *History,* 2013, [online] http://www.history.com/topics/korean-war. Accessed April 10, 2013.

32. Ibid.

33. "Vietnam War," *History,* 2013, [online] http://www.history.com/topics/vietnam-war. Accessed April 10, 2013.

34. Ibid.

35. "U.S., China Mark 30th Anniversary of Normalized Relations," *Voice of America,* October 27, 2009, [online] http://www.voanews.com/content/a-13-2008-12-15-voa39-66618542/556463.html. Accessed April 17, 2013.

36. Margaret MacMillan, *Nixon and Mao: The Week That Changed the World* (New York: Random House, 2007), pp. xvi–xxii.

37. "The Obama Administration's Pivot to Asia," *The Foreign Policy Initiative,* 2010, [online] http://www.foreignpolicyi.org/content/obama-administrations-pivot-asia. Accessed April 17, 2013.

SIX

Conclusion and Policy Recommendations

The previous chapters have demonstrated the complexities of the conflict over the South China Sea and its global ramifications. Chapter 1 lays out each nation's claims to the SCS and the various naval standoffs that have occurred because of their conflicting desires for ownership. Chapter 2 provides an analysis of the significance of the oil and natural gas industry in the region and how the rapidly growing demand for energy resources is vastly outpacing oil production. This need for resources has forced several nations in the SCS region to do business with some very questionable regimes in various parts of the world. The third chapter discusses the economic significance of the nations in the region, and it demonstrates how several countries, including the United States, have major investments in these nations and have become very dependent on Asia not only for consumer goods but also as a potential new market for their own nation's products.

The fourth chapter critiques the rise of Chinese naval power and the motives behind this development. The chapter shows how China has evolved from a largely land-based military force to a navel-based military; specifically, it is now a country with the largest naval fleet in Asia. The chapter also discusses how China has proven its ability to project itself in the open seas with its naval patrols off the coast of Somalia and its rescue of Chinese nationals during the Libyan civil war. The fifth chapter provides an overview of U.S. interest in the Asian region over the last century. The chapter covers major events, such as World War II, the Korean War, and the Vietnam War, in order to demonstrate the deep military involvement the United States has had in the region. The chapter concludes by analyzing how U.S. interest in the region has evolved from a defense focus as during World War II and the Cold War to an economic focus. This change has transformed U.S. policy in the region and given the nation a very unique outlook on the South China Sea dispute. The final chapter outlines the significance of the conflict, examines the various efforts that have been made to resolve the territorial disputes in the SCS, and provides policy recommendations to bring about its resolution.

WHY THE SOUTH CHINA SEA MATTERS

The limited amount of international intervention in the region has caused there to be very little global awareness of the conflict in the SCS region. Even within the area itself, the issue is not the most significant matter on many nations' political agenda. Therefore, why is this an issue that needs to be resolved? In order to answer this question properly, two other questions need to be addressed: (1) Currently, are there enough resources available to sustain Asia's rapid economic growth, and (2) if substantial amounts of new energy resources are not made available, how will the global economy be impacted?

When attempting to answer the energy resource question, one must first analyze the demographics of the region. Studying China, Indonesia, and Vietnam, the three most populous countries in the region, shows that there are some serious problems on the horizon. China has a population of 1.3 billion people, and the increase in its urban population is estimated at approximately 2.3 percent annually. This growth equates to an annual increase in China's urban population of approximately thirty million per year. The nation currently reports that 47 percent of its population lives in urban areas. If this number were to increase to the global average of 50 percent, then China would have over 650 million people living in cities. This enormous shift would require massive increases in energy resources.[1]

Vietnam also faces similar demographic pressures. Though not as large as China, Vietnam has a relatively large population of 92 million people and is urbanizing at a pace of 3 percent a year. This growth brings approximately 2.7 million more people into the cities each year, contributing to the spike in energy consumption. Additionally, Vietnam's population is only 30 percent urbanized, leaving massive room for growth. Indonesia, the second most populous nation in the region, also contains a large urban population. Forty-four percent of its population, or approximately 110 million Indonesians, live in urban areas. Even taking into account its modest urbanization rate of 1.7 percent, Indonesia is still adding more than four million people to its urban centers each year.[2]

The three nations mentioned are just a few examples that only scratch the surface of the depth of this problem. Such nations as Taiwan that have a modest-sized population but no sources of energy will continue to place strains on the global energy markets. The continued industrialization of countries in the region will also contribute greatly to the amount of energy consumed.

For the last decade, China has been the main destination for foreign direct investment (FDI). Its seemingly endless supply of cheap labor and ability to produce consumer products on a massive scale have created huge profit margins for investors. However, recent changes in Chinese labor conditions have caused a slight shift in investment strategies in the country. The gradual increase of wages has created a budding middle class in the nation. Companies are now repositioning themselves to be prepared for the day when China transitions from an export-oriented economy to a consumption-based one.[3]

These investments have created great opportunities for several Southeast Asian nations. FDI in Thailand rose 67 percent in 2012, and Indonesia saw an amazing 27-percent increase in investment in its nation. Vietnam is viewed as the most advanced of the new destinations for low-cost manufacturing, and several companies, such as Italian synthetic leather maker Coronet Spa, has commenced operations in Vietnam. Japan has also made major investments in both Vietnam and Indonesia and is continuing to diversify its investments in the region. Another major manufacturing operation with plans to relocate to Vietnam is Wintek Corporation, which makes electronic components for smartphones. The company announced plans in 2012 to invest 930 million dollars in four new plants that will produce displays and touch screens.[4]

Indonesia's share of FDI increased greatly following the nation's upgrade from Moody's and Fitch to an investment grade. Its growing middle class is creating a new market that several companies are seeking to tap into. Automobile makers, such as Toyota, Honda, and Nissan, plan to invest hundreds of millions of dollars in the country to boost their production. Additionally, in 2012, foreign corporations invested 4.3 billion dollars in Indonesia's mining industry.[5]

These and numerous other examples demonstrate the consistent economic growth nations in the South China Sea enjoy. In order to sustain this and continue the process of transforming their respective nations into fully developed countries, each will need a steady and reliable access to energy resources. This goal cannot be achieved with the resources contained within each respective country. Several new sources of energy will need to be brought into the marketplace to feed Asia's rapid growth alone. Also, if the growth in energy consumption in American and other emerging nations is factored in, it is clear that something needs to be done to free up the resources in the South China Sea region.

INTERNATIONAL MEDIATION EFFORTS

Despite the fact that the SCS region is of critical importance to the entire world, there has been very little international intervention aimed at resolving the issue. The majority of the governing legislation has been developed by such regional organizations as ASEAN and other bilateral or multilateral treaties. Nations such as China believe that any internationalization of the issue will cause China to lose out, so it prefers to attempt to handle all negotiations on a bilateral basis. Despite China's efforts to dictate the process for resolution, the United States and ASEAN have each been involved in helping to resolve the conflict.

United States

As mentioned in the previous chapter, the United States was engaged in several military battles in Southeast Asia in its attempts to defeat the Japanese during World War II. Several land- and maritime-based attacks were launched until a decisive victory was reached in 1945. The United States continued to monitor the area closely during the Cold War era through its naval presence in Guam and the Philippines and periodically intervened in conflicts that it viewed as threats to American national security. One of the most notable examples of this occurred during the Taiwan Straits crisis. The ultimate goal of the United States was to prevent the spread of communism in Southeast Asia, and this continued to be the main driver of U.S. policy until the fall of the Soviet Union.

As U.S. interest in the region shifted from a focus on defeating the Japanese and pursuing its containment policies to ensuring the stability of its economic interest, there have been shifts in its policy toward the SCS conflict. The Obama administration has made what it terms a "strategic pivot" toward Asia and has made several strong statements on the SCS conflict. One statement the Obama administration made that drew immediate concern was its commitment to have 60 percent of its naval assets in the SCS region. China views this increased naval presence as an aggressive attempt to counter China's influence in the region. Also, this military move could embolden such smaller nations as the Philippines and Vietnam to make more provocative moves if they believe that the United States will continue to support them no matter what.[6]

The United States has also begun to be much more vocal about its stances on issues in the SCS. The lack of any sustained naval conflicts has allowed dialogue to be the main avenue of resolving this conflict. In 2010, former Secretary of State Hillary Clinton stated that free passage in the SCS was a U.S. national interest. These comments led many to speculate on exactly what the United States was willing to do to protect this particular interest.[7]

The official stance of the United States has been one of neutrality in the conflict. The nation has only insisted that countries negotiate in good faith and come to a peaceful resolution to the conflict. The United States has been very hands off in the conflict but occasionally makes statements on the issue. In 2012, one of these statements concerning the establishment of Sansha City sparked a new controversy. The Chinese had established a government there, and the city contained a population of roughly more than one thousand people. China has also used its establishment of a governing body in the area as a gateway to extending its maritime presence in the surrounding waters. China designated Sansha a prefectural-level city, and the city is responsible for governing the Spratly and Paracel Islands and the Macclesfield Bank, which China claims.[8]

The establishment of the city has put China at odds with Vietnam, the Philippines, and other nations in the region who deem its actions as a violation of international law. The United States condemned China's actions, labeling it a "unilateral" move that will damage mediation efforts in the region. China has responded to the United States' criticism of Sansha by stating that the nations involved would be able to peacefully resolve the issue if they were not burdened with unnecessary international intervention.[9]

The United States has held strong to its principles of attempting to encourage a peaceful resolution of the SCS conflict. In recent years, most of the nation's efforts have been diplomatic and focus on attempting to serve as a counterbalance to Chinese hegemony. These efforts have been effective in preventing a large-scale naval standoff but have failed to force the nations involved in the conflict to negotiate in order to resolve their disputes. Facilitating negotiations has largely become the responsibility of such regional organizations as ASEAN.

ASEAN

ASEAN has been on the forefront of the SCS conflict since its inception. The regional grouping was formed in 1967 with five original members and has added an additional five over the last four decades. Its current members are Indonesia, Malaysia, the Philippines, Singapore, Thailand, Brunei, Burma, Cambodia, Laos, and Vietnam. China is not a member of ASEAN but is frequently involved in the negotiations with nations in the regional grouping.

The first major treaty signed involving nations in the region was the Treaty of Amity and Cooperation in Southeast Asia, which was signed in 1976. In 1995, the Treaty on the Southeast Asia Nuclear-Weapon-Free Zone was signed into law to prevent the proliferation of nuclear weapons in the region. The guiding principles behind all of these laws were to settle differences with peaceful means, to not threaten or use force against other nations, and to cooperate among the nations in economic affairs.[10]

ASEAN first became involved in the SCS dispute in response to the conflicts between Vietnam and China over territory and remained active for decades in its attempts to develop an agreement. In 2002, the goal of signing an agreement was finally reached when China agreed to sign the Declaration on the Conduct of Parties (DOC) in the South China Sea. This piece of legislation is the current legal framework used to settle disputes in the region but has been limited in its ability to force nations, particularly China, into negotiations.[11]

Military analysts have speculated that China only signed the declaration to quell fears about its increased military spending. China has been consistent about not entering into binding international agreements and has instead used its comparative advantage to negotiate with individual nations. China also was concerned about the increased military cooperation between Southeast Asian nations and the United States following 9/11 and sought to create legislation through ASEAN that would limit the United States' ability to project its power in the region. China's unwillingness to compromise and fully cooperate with the concepts in ASEAN's DOC has made the legislation ineffective and limited its ability to enforce peace in the region.[12]

RECOMMENDATIONS

The conflict over the territory in the South China Sea region has continued for decades with very little signs of a possible resolution. The concluding section of the book outlines four key policy recommendations that, if implemented, could greatly enhance the chances of ending the stalemate.

Revisions of International Maritime Law

The United Nations passed the current international maritime legal framework—the United Nations Convention on the Law of the Sea (UNCLOS)—in 1982 after over two decades of debate. The bases of the laws were conceptualized in 1958 at a time when the world was in a very different state. Large portions of the globe were still under some form of colonial or indirect rule, and few could predict that this treaty would make the international maritime system become even more chaotic.[13]

The most significant challenge is the advancements in offshore oil drilling technologies. In the first half of the twentieth century, nations primarily focused all of their resources on mainland exploration and were able to discover an abundance of resources. Over time, however, as the world continued to develop, global demand for energy shot through the roof. In addition to this increase in demand, environmental conservation efforts launched in western nations caused a slowdown in exploration and exploitation of new energy resources.

Investors took these factors into consideration and began to devote more resources to offshore operations. As companies discovered large-scale deposits and made profits, they continued to expand their operations. The technology currently exists for deep-sea oil exploration, but the question that remains is how to determine who owns these resources. With the ever-increasing ability of corporations to drill farther and farther offshore, nations have been eager to extend the length of their exclusive economic zones.

Another issue that current international law fails to take into account is the fragmented nature and proximity of the island nations. In the South China Sea region, several countries have dozens of small islands that significantly extend the ends of their borders. The border issue is one of the main contributing factors to the overlapping claims within the area. For instance, Malaysia, Indonesia, and Brunei are each virtually the same distance from the Spratly Islands. Also, China and Vietnam are roughly the same distance from the Paracel Islands, making conflicting claims an unavoidable reality. There are also several other miniature land masses in the sea that various nations are attempting to claim to solidify more lucrative interest.

With these concerns in mind, policymakers should revise international law so that the official end of a nation's territory and beginning of its territorial waters is a place that is significantly integrated into the rest of the nation. An example of this integration occurs with the Hawaiian Islands, which are very far from mainland United States, but the islands house military installations, attract millions of American tourists, and host plenty of major American sporting events. Therefore, the islands are a substantive part of the United States and are a reasonable boundary for the country. A similar criterion needs to be developed for nations in the South China Sea in order to differentiate between the legitimate and illegitimate claims.

Encourage Economic Cooperation and Strengthen Regional Organizations

The necessity of increased access to sources of energy makes it highly unlikely that any nation will voluntarily denounce its claims to the sea or agree to any sort of winner-take-all arbitration efforts. As discussed in the previous suggestion, the close proximity of nations in the SCS makes overlapping claims an unavoidable reality, and at the present time, it is extremely difficult to evaluate the validity of claims. Another unpopular but virtually indisputable fact is that none of the nations in the region have the capability to fully exploit the resources contained within their territories on their own.

To fully maximize the economic output of the area, the nations need to make a significant amount of regional exploration agreements. The resources are spread out in an expansive area, so surveying and assessing will be very costly. Multinationals, such as Exxon Mobile and BP, have operations in several countries and could be used as the conduits for cooperative efforts in the region.

Additionally, the countries involved should take measures to encourage interregional trade. Presently, the majority of the countries in the region have strong trading relationships with China, and the smaller nations should expand their trading relations so they can trade among themselves. Hopefully, increasing the amount of trade and movement of goods and people will lessen the significance of national borders and foster a spirit of cooperation among nations in the region.

ASEAN is the most significant regional body in the South China Sea region. It has made several attempts to mediate the conflict; one of those efforts was the creation of the 2002 Code of Conduct. Its main challenge has been its inability to force nations to abide by its principles. Although China signed the Code of Conduct, it is not an ASEAN member. This limits the organization's ability to influence China's actions. Some nations within ASEAN also have disproportionate economic power and political influence, making it impossible for smaller countries to reach a fair deal in bilateral negotiations.[14]

This point highlights the significant role regional organizations should play in resolving this dispute. With all the varying conflicting claims, the countries will need to develop a broad-based consensus in order to come to any type of sustainable resolution. Strengthening both regional economic cooperation and regional organizations has the potential to provide a pathway to peace and is therefore strongly recommended.

Resolving the Taiwan–China Issue

Ever since the communist government forced Chang Kai-Shek's KMT government to flee from mainland China to the island of Formosa, there has been a constant threat of maritime-based warfare between the two sides. For years, Mao Xedong's People's Republic of China (PRC) was isolated and unable to gain recognition as the legitimate government of mainland China. There were several standoffs in the straits of Taiwan, and the United States often times deployed military personnel to support to the Taiwanese government. As Cold War–era rivalries began to shift, relations between the PRC and the United States began to improve, eventually leading to recognition in 1979. The United States pledged its commitment to continuing its defense of the people of Taiwan and has continued to sell weapons to its government to defend itself from any Chinese aggression. These moves have essentially neutralized the two sides and led to a seemingly endless standoff.[15]

The unrecognized status of Taiwan has also made the SCS conflict much more complex. Taiwan has essentially been forced to agree with China's claims in an effort to keep from jeopardizing its own status. China has been very hesitant to make any concessions that could eventually be used as a precedent for Taiwan's independence. The rivalry has also caused an increased militarization of the region. Both Taiwan and China have committed large amounts of their budgets to defense and the purchase of new equipment. This militarization has made other neighboring countries nervous and could eventually force all of the nations to increase their spending. It is recommended that the nations involved make some sort of permanent decision in regards to the status of Taiwan. Having the nation in a constant state of limbo brings uncertainty to the region and impedes mediation efforts.

Pressure China to Negotiate

In any objective analysis of the SCS dispute, it becomes very clear that China is the main propagandistic force at work. China claims the entire SCS based upon historic maps and refuses to quantify its claims to the sea in any specific terms. China also refuses to sincerely take part in multilateral negotiations and instead has opted to attempt to use its power to force smaller nations into unfavorable deals. The biggest concern is that of all the nations in the region, China is the one who truly needs the energy resources the most. Other nations view these resources as a new potential source of revenue for their countries' development; however, China sees those same resources as crucial for its continued prosperity. Additionally, the smaller, less-advanced nations in the region do not have the capital necessary to finance the exploration and extraction of the resources. This has made them more willing to work together and negotiate a plan to jointly develop the area.

China, on the other hand, has an abundance of capital and is fully capable of financing the extraction of resources in the SCS. Additionally, China has and will continue to have a devastating shortage of energy supplies for its rapidly industrializing and massively populated country. Arguably, the most significant point is that the oil that China imports is coming from some of the most volatile places on earth. Some of China's largest suppliers include Sudan, Nigeria, and several countries across the Middle East. These countries have suffered from political unrest and, in the case of Nigeria and Sudan, have seen production facilities attacked by insurgent elements.[16]

This instability has caused spikes in prices and put China's steady supply of resources in jeopardy. Another factor that is a major cause of concern for China is the shipping lanes that its oil supply has to travel through. The majority of China's energy resources reaches the nation after traveling through the SCS and could easily be cut off by rival countries. Therefore, China not only views the sea as a potential resource, but it also views the islands as strategic points of interest to ensure the safe delivery of its supplies of energy. In sum, the stakes in the SCS are so much higher for China that it is very unlikely the country will be willing to compromise.

This reality should cause nations like the United States to strongly analyze the support it continues to give to China. The steady flow of foreign investment into China and the insatiable demand for its exports is creating the revenue that allows China's antagonistic stances in the SCS. If a peaceful resolution to the ongoing dispute in the SCS is a priority for the United States, then the United States needs to place economic pressure on China to get it to negotiate. Also, other powers in the region, for example, Japan and India, have the ability to counter China's strong influence. Nearly every country involved in the SCS dispute counts Japan as one of its top trading partners, giving the nation the opportunity to be an alternative hegemonic force. India, with its strong economy and active navy, also has potential to have a strong influence in the region.[17]

CONCLUSION

As the book has demonstrated, the conflict in the South China Sea is primarily driven by economic and political concerns. Nations have taken hard-line stances on the issue over the last few decades in an effort to position themselves to exploit the resources. The only viable resolution to the conflict, short of naval warfare, is joint economic development programs and regional cooperation. The majority of the countries have been receptive to this idea, but as of this writing, China has refused to accept any plans that impede on its claim. Until China can be neutralized, the conflict will continue to spiral on with periodic small-scale naval skirmishes and possibly an escalation of hostilities. It will be up to the United States, the United Nations, and other major powers to decide where the conflict falls on the list of international priorities and act accordingly. If a sustained effort is made to force all the parties involved to specifically quantify their claims and come to some sort of negotiation in which all can benefit, a nonviolent resolution is very possible. The benefits of peaceful exploration and exploitation of the resources in the SCS would be a tremendous boon not only to the region but also the entire world. With this in mind, every effort should be made to bring this standoff to an end and usher in an era of peace and prosperity in the region.

NOTES

1. Central Intelligence Agency, "China," *World Factbook*, 2013, [online] https://www.cia.gov/library/publications/the-world-factbook/geos/ch.html. Accessed March 29, 2013.

2. Central Intelligence Agency, "Vietnam," *World Factbook*, 2013, [online] https://www.cia.gov/library/publications/the-world-factbook/geos/vm.html. Accessed March 29, 2013; Central Intelligence Agency, "Indonesia," *World Factbook*, 2013, [online] https://www.cia.gov/library/publications/the-world-factbook/geos/id.html. Accessed March 29, 2013.

3. Dan Steinbock, "Foreign Investment Relocates in China and Asia," *EconoMonitor*, February 27, 2013, [online] http://www.economonitor.com/blog/2013/02/foreign-investment-relocates-in-china-and-asia. Accessed April 19, 2013.

4. "China Begins to Lose Edge as World's Factory Floor," *Wall Street Journal*, January 16, 2013, [online] http://online.wsj.com/article/SB10001424127887323783704578245241751969774.html. Accessed April 19, 2013.

5. Made Sentana, "Indonesia Foreign Direct Investment Hits High," *Wall Street Journal*, January 22, 2013, [online] http://online.wsj.com/article/SB10001424127887324624404578257212289247592.html. Accessed April 19, 2013.

6. Robert Tofani, "Ambiguity Afloat in the South China Sea," *Asia Times*, April 24, 2013, [online] http://www.atimes.com/atimes/Southeast_Asia/SEA-01-240413.html. Accessed April 25, 2013.

7. Ibid.

8. Alexa Olesen, "Shansha, China's New 'City,' Strengthens Country's Foothold in Disputed Waters," *The Huffington Post*, July 24, 2012, [online] http://www.huffingtonpost.com/2012/07/24/sansha-china_n_1697523.html. Accessed April 25, 2013.

9. Brian Spegel, "New Tensions Rise on the South China Sea," *Wall Street Journal*, August 5, 2012, [online] http://online.wsj.com/article/SB10000872396390443659204577570514282930558.html. Accessed April 25, 2013.

10. Tran Truong Thuy, "Recent Developments in the South China Sea: Implications for Regional Security and Cooperation," *Center for Strategic and International Studies, Southeast Asia Program*, n.d., pp. 3–5, [online] http://csis.org/files/publication/110629_Thuy_South_China_Sea.pdf. Accessed April 26, 2013.

11. "Declaration on the Conduct of Parties in the South China Sea," *Association of Southeast Asian Nations*, 2012, [online] http://www.asean.org/asean/external-relations/china/item/declaration-on-the-conduct-of-parties-in-the-south-china-sea. Accessed April 26, 2013.

12. Thuy, pp. 5–7.

13. Peter Malanczuk, *Akehurst's Modern Introduction to International Law* (New York: Routledge, 1997), pp. 173–74.

14. Rodolfo Severino, "A Code of Conduct for the South China Sea," *Center for Strategic and International Studies*, PacNet, Number 45A, August 17, 2012.

15. "A Country Study: China," *Library of Congress Country Studies*, August 24, 2012, [online] http://lcweb2.loc.gov/frd/cs/cntoc.html. Accessed March 24, 2013.

16. Christopher Alessi and Stephanie Hanson, "Expanding China–Africa Oil Ties," *Council on Foreign Relations*, February 8, 2012, [online] http://www.cfr.org/china/expanding-china-africa-oil-ties/p9557. Accessed April 21, 2013.

17. Karl Lester M. Yap, "Abe's Japanese Stimulus Seen Boosting Southeast Asia," *Bloomberg News*, January 20, 2013, [online] http://www.bloomberg.com/news/2013-01-20/japan-s-stimulus-seen-boosting-southeast-asia-as-korea-suffers.html. Accessed April 21, 2013.

Appendix A
Timeline of Key Events

1899 U.S.–Philippine War

1941 Japanese launch attack on Pearl Harbor; Guam attacked and seized by Japanese forces

1944 Guam reclaimed by America

1945 Atomic bomb used on Japan, leading to its surrender in World War II

1946 Philippines granted independence; China claims Spratly Islands as a part of its Guandong Province

1949 United States ends diplomatic ties with China

1950 Guam Organic Act signed; Korean War

1951 Japan relinquishes claims to South China Sea

1954 United States signs mutual defense treaty with Taiwan

1955 First Taiwan Straits crisis

1958 Second Taiwan Straits crisis

1965 U.S. ground troops deployed to fight in Vietnam

1972 President Richard Nixon meets with Mao Zedong in China

1973 United States withdrawals troops from Vietnam

1974 China captures Paracel Islands; naval standoff between China and Vietnam

1975 Reunification of Northern and Southern Vietnam

1979 Normalization of relations between the United States and China (PRC)

1982 Signing of the United Nations Convention on the Law of the Sea

1988 Vietnamese sailors killed by Chinese navy in Johnson South Reef Skirmish

1991 China claims entire South China Sea on the basis of international law

1995 Third Taiwan Straits crisis; China and the Philippines battle over Mischief Reef

2000 Philippine troops kill Chinese fishermen

2002 China and ASEAN nations sign Declaration on the Code of Conduct of Parties in the South China Sea

2011 United States condemns China's use of force in the South China Sea and commences naval drills with Vietnam; ExxonMobil discovers oil off the coast of Vietnam

2012 United States announces plans to shift 60 percent of its naval assets to the Pacific by 2020

Appendix B

Key People and Institutions

KEY PEOPLE

Eisenhower, Dwight: Won the presidency of the United States in 1953 and remained in office until 1961. During his tenure the United States concluded its military involvement in the Korean War. The United States also signed a mutual defense treaty with Taiwan during his administration.

Jintao, Hu: President of the People's Republic of China from 2003 to 2013; during his term China experienced rapid economic growth and developed a much more formidable military. China also became more aggressive in protecting its claims in the South China Sea under his administration.

Lee Teng-hui: Was the first democratically elected president of Taiwan. His visit to the United States in 1995 sparked the third Taiwan Straits crisis.

MacArthur, Douglas: One of the most prominent leaders of American armed forces in the Pacific theater of World War II. In 1941 he became commander of the U.S. Army Forces in the Far East and oversaw the occupation of Japan. He remained a prominent leader within the military until he was removed from his command by President Harry Truman.

Obama, Barack: Current president of the United States. Under his administration the United States announced a strategic "pivot" to Asia, which involves stationing 60 percent of the nation's naval assets in the Pacific.

Ramos, Fidel V.: Served as president of the Philippines from 1992 to 1998. During his time in office, the Philippines and China had a major military standoff over Mischief Reef.

Roosevelt, Franklin: President of the United States from 1933 until his death in 1945. Roosevelt signed the declaration of war against Japan in 1941 and ordered U.S. troops into several different conflicts in the Pacific theater.

Shek, Chiang Kai: Ruled both mainland China and Taiwan over the course of his political career. During his time as head of state in mainland China, he fought against the Japanese invasion. He was eventually forced from power by Mao Zedong's communist forces and fled to Taiwan, where he was in power until the time of his death in 1975.

Truman, Harry: Served as president of the United States from 1945 to 1953. During his administration the United States adopted the Truman Doctrine, which sought to contain the spread of communism. During his time in office, the United States used atomic bombs to force Japan to surrender and also engaged in the Korean conflict.

Xiaoping, Deng: Was the paramount leader of China from 1978 to 1992. During his time in leadership, China reestablished its relationship with the United States and opened its economy to foreign investments. He also oversaw the beginning stages of the modernization of China's military and naval forces.

Zedong, Mao: Led China's communist revolution and governed the country from 1949 to the time of his death. During the majority of Mao's reign as head of the People's Republic of China, the nation was isolated from the United States, but relations improved following a meeting with President Nixon in 1972.

KEY INSTITUTIONS

Asia Pacific Economic Cooperation (APEC): Founded in 1989 with the goal of increasing economic cooperation between member nations. It currently has twenty-one members and represents one of the largest trading blocks in the world.

Association of Southeast Asian Nations (ASEAN): Formed in 1967 with five original members and has added an additional five over the last four decades. Its current members are Indonesia, Malaysia, the Philippines, Singapore, Thailand, Brunei, Burma, Cambodia, Laos, and Vietnam. ASEAN has been the leading international actor in the South China Sea negotiations.

China National Offshore Oil Corp (CNOOC): CNOOC is the third-largest oil company in China and was established to exploit China's offshore oil and gas resources. The company is the nation's main operator in the South China Sea, and in 2010 it was producing 800,000 barrels of crude oil per day domestically and an additional 200,000 overseas.

Chinese National Petroleum Corporation (CNPC): CNPC was established in 1988 and has developed into a major energy company with both upstream and downstream interest. The company is also involved in logistics and manufacturing and managing technical services for energy development projects. In 2010 the company's domestic crude oil production was 2.1 million barrels a day and 72.5 billion cubic meters of gas annually. CNPC also has extensive overseas operation and is internationally listed on stock exchanges under its subsidiary, PetroChina.

Chinese Petroleum Corporation (CPC): Established in 1946 in Shanghai and relocated to Taiwan after the communist revolution on the mainland. CPC is a state-owned entity that dominates all segments of Taiwan's energy industry.

Petronas: A wholly state-owned Malaysian enterprise that is one of the world's largest corporations. Petronas holds exclusive ownership rights to all exploration and production projects in the nation, and all foreign and private companies must form joint agreements with them to operate within the country. In addition to its exclusive production rights in Malaysia, it also has global operations in Asia, Africa, Australia, Europe, and North and South America.

Petrovietnam: The government-owned oil company of the Vietnamese government. The company accounts for 20 percent of the oil and 50 percent of the nation's gas production. Petrovietnam also has several joint ventures with international firms.

Philippine National Oil Company (PNOC): A government-run holding company that has subsidiaries operating in each sector of the nation's oil and natural gas industry. It was established in 1976 and has been the leading actor in the country's energy sector since its inception.

Appendix C

International Treaties Involving
Nations in the South China Sea Region

POTSDAM DECLARATION, JULY 26, 1945

Defining Terms for Japanese Surrender
  Issued on July 26, 1945, at the Potsdam Conference in Potsdam, Germany

1. We, the President of the United States, the President of the National Government of the Republic of China, and the Prime Minister of Great Britain, representing the hundreds of millions of our countrymen, have conferred and agree that Japan shall be given an opportunity to end this war.
2. The prodigious land, sea and air forces of the United States, the British Empire and of China, many times reinforced by their armies and air fleets from the west, are poised to strike the final blows upon Japan. This military power is sustained and inspired by the determination of all the Allied Nations to prosecute the war against Japan until she ceases to resist.
3. The result of the futile and senseless German resistance to the might of the aroused free peoples of the world stands forth in awful clarity as an example to the people of Japan. The might that now converges on Japan is immeasurably greater than that which, when applied to the resisting Nazis, necessarily laid waste to the lands, the industry and the method of life of the whole German people. The full application of our military power, backed by our resolve, will mean the inevitable and complete destruction of the Japanese armed forces and just as inevitably the utter devastation of the Japanese homeland.
4. The time has come for Japan to decide whether she will continue to be controlled by those self-willed militaristic advisers whose unin-

telligent calculations have brought the Empire of Japan to the threshold of annihilation, or whether she will follow the path of reason.

5. Following are our terms. We will not deviate from them. There are no alternatives. We shall brook no delay.

6. There must be eliminated for all time the authority and influence of those who have deceived and misled the people of Japan into embarking on world conquest, for we insist that a new order of peace, security and justice will be impossible until irresponsible militarism is driven from the world.

7. Until such a new order is established and until there is convincing proof that Japan's war-making power is destroyed, points in Japanese territory to be designated by the Allies shall be occupied to secure the achievement of the basic objectives we are here setting forth.

8. The terms of the Cairo Declaration shall be carried out and Japanese sovereignty shall be limited to the islands of Honshu, Hokkaido, Kyushu, Shikoku and such minor islands as we determine.

9. The Japanese military forces, after being completely disarmed, shall be permitted to return to their homes with the opportunity to lead peaceful and productive lives.

10. We do not intend that the Japanese shall be enslaved as a race or destroyed as a nation, but stern justice shall be meted out to all war criminals, including those who have visited cruelties upon our prisoners. The Japanese Government shall remove all obstacles to the revival and strengthening of democratic tendencies among the Japanese people. Freedom of speech, of religion, and of thought, as well as respect for the fundamental human rights shall be established.

11. Japan shall be permitted to maintain such industries as will sustain her economy and permit the exaction of just reparations in kind, but not those which would enable her to re-arm for war. To this end, access to, as distinguished from control of, raw materials shall be permitted. Eventual Japanese participation in world trade relations shall be permitted.

12. The occupying forces of the Allies shall be withdrawn from Japan as soon as these objectives have been accomplished and there has been established in accordance with the freely expressed will of the Japanese people a peacefully inclined and responsible government.

13. We call upon the government of Japan to proclaim now the unconditional surrender of all Japanese armed forces, and to provide proper and adequate assurances of their good faith in such action. The alternative for Japan is prompt and utter destruction.

TREATY OF MUTUAL COOPERATION AND SECURITY BETWEEN THE UNITED STATES OF AMERICA AND JAPAN, JANUARY 19, 1960

Signed at Washington, January 19, 1960
  Approved by the diet, June 19, 1960
  Ratification decided by the cabinet, June 21, 1960
  Attested, June 21, 1960
  Ratifications exchanged at Tokyo, June 23, 1960
  Promulgated, June 23, 1960
  Entered into force, June 23, 1960

Japan and the United States of America,

Desiring to strengthen the bonds of peace and friendship traditionally existing between them, and to uphold the principles of democracy, individual liberty, and the rule of law,

Desiring further to encourage closer economic cooperation between them and to promote conditions of economic stability and well being in their countries,

Reaffirming their faith in the purposes and principles of the Charter of the United Nations, and their desire to live in peace with all peoples and all governments,

Recognizing that they have the inherent right of individual or collective self-defense as affirmed in the Charter of the United Nations,

Considering that they have a common concern in the maintenance of international peace and security in the Far East,

Having resolved to conclude a treaty of mutual cooperation and security

Therefore agree as follows:

Article 1

The Parties undertake, as set forth in the Charter of the United Nations, to settle any international disputes in which they may be involved by peaceful means in such a manner that international peace and security and justice are not endangered and to refrain in their international relations from the threat or use of force against the territorial integrity or political independence of any state, or in any other manner inconsistent with the purposes of the United Nations.

The Parties will endeavor in concert with other peace loving countries to strengthen the United Nations so that its mission of maintaining international peace and security may be discharged more effectively.

Article 2

The Parties will contribute toward the further development of peaceful and friendly international relations by strengthening their free institutions, by bringing about a better understanding of the principles upon which these institutions are founded, and by promoting conditions of stability and well being. They will seek to eliminate conflict in their international economic policies and will encourage economic collaboration between them.

Article 3

The Parties, individually and in cooperation with each other, by means of continuous and effective self-help and mutual aid will maintain and develop, subject to their constitutional provisions, their capacities to resist armed attack.

Article 4

The Parties will consult together from time to time regarding the implementation of this Treaty, and, at the request of either Party, whenever the security of Japan or international peace and security in the Far East is threatened.

Article 5

Each Party recognizes that an armed attack against either Party in the territories under the administration of Japan would be dangerous to its own peace and safety and declares that it would act to meet the common danger in accordance with its constitutional provisions and processes.

Any such armed attack and all measures taken as a result thereof shall be immediately reported to the Security Council of the United Nations in accordance with the provisions of Article 51 of the Charter. Such measures shall be terminated when the Security Council has taken the measures necessary to restore and maintain international peace and security.

Article 6

For the purpose of contributing to the security of Japan and the maintenance of international peace and security in the Far East, the United States of America is granted the use by its land, air and naval forces of facilities and areas in Japan.

The use of these facilities and areas as well as the status of United States armed forces in Japan shall be governed by a separate agreement, replacing the Administrative Agreement under Article III of the Security Treaty between Japan and the United States of America, signed at Tokyo on February 28, 1952, as amended, and by such other arrangements as may be agreed upon.

Article 7

This Treaty does not affect and shall not be interpreted as affecting in any way the rights and obligations of the Parties under the Charter of the United Nations or the responsibility of the United Nations for the maintenance of international peace and security.

Article 8

This Treaty shall be ratified by Japan and the United States of America in accordance with their respective constitutional processes and will enter into force on the date on which the instruments of ratification thereof have been exchanged by them in Tokyo.

Article 9

The Security Treaty between Japan and the United States of America signed at the city of San Francisco on September 8, 1951, shall expire upon the entering into force of this Treaty.

Article 10

This Treaty shall remain in force until in the opinion of the Governments of Japan and the United States of America there shall have come into force such United Nations arrangements as will satisfactorily provide for the maintenance of international peace and security in the Japan area.

However, after the Treaty has been in force for ten years, either Party may give notice to the other Party of its intention to terminate the Treaty, in which case the Treaty shall terminate one year after such notice has been given.

IN WITNESS WHEREOF the undersigned Plenipotentiaries have signed this Treaty. DONE in duplicate at Washington in the Japanese and English languages, both equally authentic, this 19th day of January, 1960.

For Japan:
Nobusuke Kishi
Auchiro Fujiyama
Mitsujiro Ishii
Tadashi Adachi
Koichiro Asakai

For the United States of America:
Christian A. Herter
Douglas MacArthur 2nd
J. Graham Parson

MUTUAL DEFENSE TREATY BETWEEN THE UNITED STATES OF AMERICA AND THE REPUBLIC OF CHINA, DECEMBER 2, 1954

The Parties to this Treaty,

Reaffirming their faith in the purposes and principles of the Charter of the United Nations and their desire to live in peace with all peoples and all Governments, and desiring to strengthen the fabric of peace in the West Pacific Area,

Recalling with mutual pride the relationship which brought their two peoples together in a common bond of sympathy and mutual ideals to fight side by side against imperialist aggression during the last war,

Desiring to declare publicly and formally their sense of unity and their common determination to defend themselves against external armed attack, so that no potential aggressor could be under the illusion that either of them stands alone in the West Pacific Area, and

Desiring further to strengthen their present efforts for collective defense for the preservation of peace and security pending the development of a more comprehensive system of regional security in the West Pacific Area,

Have agreed as follows:

Article 1

The Parties undertake, as set forth in the Charter of the United Nations, to settle any international dispute in which they may be involved by peaceful means in such a manner that international peace, security and justice are not endangered and to refrain in their international relations from the threat or use of force in any manner inconsistent with the purposes of the United Nations.

Article 2

In order more effectively to achieve the objective of this Treaty, the Parties separately and jointly by self-help and mutual aid will maintain and develop their individual and collective capacity to resist armed attack and communist subversive activities directed from without against their territorial integrity and political stability.

Article 3

The Parties undertake to strengthen their free institutions and to cooperate with each other in the development of economic progress and social well-being and to further their individual and collective efforts toward these ends.

Article 4

The Parties, through their Foreign Ministers or their deputies, will consult together from time to time regarding the implementation of this Treaty.

Article 5

Each Party recognizes that an armed attack in the West Pacific Area directed against the territories of either of the Parties would be dangerous to its own peace and safety and declares that it would act to meet the common danger in accordance with its constitutional processes.

Any such armed attack and all measures taken as a result thereof shall be immediately reported to the Security Council of the United Nations. Such measures shall be terminated when the Security Council has taken the measures necessary to restore and maintain international peace and security.

Article 6

For the purposes of Articles 2 and 5, the terms "territorial" and "territories" shall mean in respect of the Republic of China, Taiwan and the Pescadores; and in respect of the United States of America, the island territories in the West Pacific under its jurisdiction. The provisions of Articles 2 and 5 will be applicable to such other territories as may be determined by mutual agreement.

Article 7

The Government of the Republic of China grants, and the Government of the United States of America accepts, the right to dispose such United States land, air, and sea forces in and about Taiwan and the Pescadores as may be required for their defense, as determined by mutual agreement.

Article 8

This Treaty does not affect and shall not be interpreted as affecting in any way the rights and obligations of the Parties under the Charter of the

United Nations or the responsibility of the United Nations for the mainte-nance of international peace and security.

Article 9

This Treaty shall be ratified by the Republic of China and the United States of America in accordance with their respective constitutional pro-cesses and will come into force when instruments of ratification thereof have been exchanged by them at Taipei.

Article 10

This Treaty shall remain in force indefinitely. Either Party may termi-nate it one year after notice has been given to the other party.

IN WITNESS WHEREOF, The undersigned Plenipotentiaries have signed this Treaty.

DONE in duplicate, in the Chinese and English languages, at Wash-ington on this Second day of the Twelfth month of the Forty-third Year of the Republic of China, corresponding to the Second day of December of the Year One Thousand Nine Hundred and Fifty-four.

For the Republic of China:
George K. C. Yeh

For the United States of America:
John Foster Dulles

U.S. Congressional Authorization for the President to Employ the Armed Forces of the United States to Protect Formosa, the Pescadores, and Relat-ed Positions and Territories of That Area

Whereas the primary purpose of the United States, in its relations with all other nations, is to develop and sustain a just and enduring peace for all; and Whereas certain territories in the West Pacific under the jurisdiction of the Republic of China are now under armed attack, and threats and declarations have been and are being made by the Chinese Communists that such armed attack is in aid of and in preparation for armed attack on Formosa and the Pescadores,

Whereas such armed attack if continued would gravely endanger the peace and security of the West Pacific Area and particularly of Formosa and the Pescadores; and

Whereas the secure possession by friendly governments of the Western Pacific Island chain, of which Formosa is a part, is essential to the vital interests of the United States and all friendly nations in or bordering upon the Pacific Ocean; and

Whereas the President of the United States on January 6, 1955, submitted to the Senate for its advice and consent to ratification a Mutual Defense Treaty between the United States of America and the Republic of China, which recognizes that an armed attack in the West Pacific Area directed against territories, therein described, in the region of Formosa and the Pescadores, would be dangerous to the peace and safety of the parties to the treaty:

Therefore be it Resolved by the Senate and House of Representatives of the United States of America in Congress assembled, That the President of the United States be and he hereby is authorized to employ the Armed Forces of the United States as he deems necessary for the specific purpose of securing and protecting Formosa and the Pescadores against armed attack, this authority to include the securing and protection of such related positions and territories of that area now in friendly hands and the taking of such other measures as he judges to be required or appropriate in assuring the defense of Formosa and the Pescadores.

This resolution shall expire when the President shall determine that the peace and security of the area is reasonably assured by international conditions created by action of the United Nations or otherwise, and shall so report to the Congress.

THE PHILIPPINE INDEPENDENCE ACT (TYDINGS–MCDUFFIE ACT), MARCH 24, 1934

An act to provide for the complete independence of the Philippine Islands, to provide for the adoption of a constitution and a form of government for the Philippine Islands, and for other purposes.

Convention to Frame Constitution for Philippine Islands

Section 1. The Philippine Legislature is hereby authorized to provide for the election of delegates to a constitutional convention, which shall meet in the hall of the House of Representatives in the capital of the Philippine Islands, at such time as the Philippine Legislature may fix, but not later than October 1, 1934, to formulate and draft a constitution for the government of the Commonwealth of the Philippine Islands, subject to the conditions and qualifications prescribed in this Act, which shall exercise jurisdiction over all the territory ceded to the United States by the treaty of peace concluded between the United States and Spain on the

10th day of December, 1898, the boundaries of which are set forth in Article III of said treaty, together with those islands embraced in the treaty between Spain and the United States concluded at Washington on the 7th day of November, 1900. The Philippine Legislature shall provide for the necessary expenses of such convention.

Character of Constitutions—Mandatory Provisions

Section 2.

(a) The constitution formulated and drafted shall be republican in form, shall contain a bill of rights, and shall, either as a part thereof or in an ordinance appended thereto, contain provisions to the effect that, pending the final and complete withdrawal of the sovereignty of the United States over the Philippine Islands—

1. All citizens of the Philippine Islands shall owe allegiance to the United States.
2. Every officer of the government of the Commonwealth of the Philippine Islands shall, before entering upon the discharge of his duties, take and subscribes an oath of office, declaring, among other things, that he recognizes and accepts the supreme authority of and will maintain true faith and allegiance to the United States.
3. Absolute toleration of religious sentiment shall be secured and no inhabitant or religious organization shall be molested in person or property on account of religious belief or mode of worship.
4. Property owned by the United States, cemeteries, churches, and parsonages or convents appurtenant thereto, and all lands, buildings, and improvements used exclusively for religious, charitable, or educational purposes shall be exempt from taxation.
5. Trade relations between the Philippine Islands and the United States shall be upon the basis prescribed in section 6.
6. The public debt of the Philippine Islands and its subordinate branches shall not exceed limits now or hereafter fixed by the Congress of the United States; and no loans shall be contracted in foreign countries without the approval of the President of the United States.
7. The debts, liabilities, and obligations of the present Philippine Government, its provinces, municipalities, and instrumentalities, valid and subsisting at the time of the adoption of the constitution, shall be assumed and paid by the new government.
8. Provision shall be made for the establishment and maintenance of an adequate system of public schools, primarily conducted in the English.

9. Acts affecting currency, coinage, imports, exports, and immigration shall not become law until approved by the President of the United States.
10. Foreign affairs shall be under the direct supervision and control of the United States.
11. All acts passed by the Legislature of the Commonwealth of the Philippine Islands shall be reported to the Congress of the United States.
12. The Philippine Islands recognizes the right of the United States to expropriate property for public uses, to maintain military and other reservations and armed forces in the Philippines, and, upon order of the President, to call into the service of such armed forces all military forces organized by the Philippine Government.
13. The decisions of the courts of the Commonwealth of the Philippine Islands shall be subject to review by the Supreme Court of the United States as provided in paragraph 6 of section 7.
14. The United States may, by Presidential proclamation, exercise the right to intervene for the preservation of the government of the Commonwealth of the Philippine Islands and for the maintenance of the government as provided in the constitution thereof, and for the protection of life, property, and individual liberty and for the discharge of government obligations under and in accordance with the provisions of the constitution.
15. The authority of the United States High Commissioner to the government of the Commonwealth of the Philippine Islands, as provided in this Act, shall be recognized.
16. Citizens and corporations of the United States shall enjoy in the Commonwealth of the Philippine Islands all the civil rights of the citizens and corporations, respectively, thereof.

(b) The constitution shall also contain the following provisions, effective as of the date of the proclamation of the President recognizing the independence of the Philippine Islands, as hereinafter provided:

1. That the property rights of the United States and the Philippine Islands shall be promptly adjusted and settled, and that all existing property rights of citizens or corporations of the United States shall be acknowledged, respected, and safeguarded to the same extent as property rights of citizens of the Philippine Islands.
2. That the officials elected and serving under the constitution adopted pursuant to the provisions of this Act shall be constitutional officers of the free and independent Government of the Philippine Islands and qualified to function in all respects as if elected

directly under such government, and shall serve their full terms of office as prescribed in the constitution.

3. That the debts and liabilities of the Philippine Islands, its provinces, cities, municipalities, and instrumentalities, which shall be valid and subsisting at the time of the final and complete withdrawal of the sovereignty of the United States, shall be assumed by the free and independent Government of the Philippine Islands; and that where bonds have been issued under authority of an Act of Congress of the United States by the Philippine Islands, or any province, city, or municipality therein, the Philippine Government will make adequate provision for the necessary funds for the payment of interest and principal, and such obligations shall be a first lien on the taxes collected in the Philippine Islands.

4. That the Government of the Philippine Islands, on becoming independent of the United States, will assume all continuing obligations assumed by the United States under the treaty of peace with Spain ceding said Philippine Islands to the United States.

5. That by way of further assurance the Government of the Philippine Islands will embody the foregoing provisions [except paragraph (2)] in a treaty with the United States.

Submission of Constitution to the President of the United States

Section 3. Upon the drafting and approval of the constitution by the constitutional convention in the Philippine Islands, the constitution shall be submitted within two years after the enactment of this Act to the President of the United States, who shall determine whether or not it conforms with the provisions of this Act. If the President finds that the proposed constitution conforms substantially with the provisions of this Act he shall so certify to the Governor-General of the Philippine Islands, who shall so advise the constitutional convention. If the President finds that the constitution does not conform with the provisions of this Act he shall so advise the Governor-General of the Philippine Islands, stating wherein in his judgment the constitution does not so conform and submitting provisions which will in his judgment make the constitution so conform. The Governor-General shall in turn submit such message to the constitutional convention for further action by them pursuant to the same procedure hereinbefore defined, until the President and the constitutional convention are in agreement.

Submission of Constitution to Filipino People

Section 4. After the President of the United States has certified that the constitution conforms with the provisions of this Act, it shall be submitted to the people of the Philippine Islands for their ratification or rejection at an election to be held within four months after the date of such certification, on a date to be fixed by the Philippine Legislature, at which election the qualified voters of the Philippine Islands shall have an opportunity to vote directly for or against the proposed constitution and ordinances appended thereto. Such election shall be held in such manner as may be prescribed by the Philippine Legislature, to which the return of the election shall be made. The Philippine Legislature shall by law provide for the canvassing of the return and shall certify the result to the Governor-General of the Philippine Islands, together with a statement of the votes cast, and a copy of said constitution and ordinances. If a majority of the votes cast shall be for the constitution, such vote shall be deemed an expression of the will of the people of the Philippine Islands in favor of Philippine independence, and the Governor-General shall, within thirty days after receipt of the certification from the Philippine Legislature, issue a proclamation for the election of officers of the government of the Commonwealth of the Philippine Islands provided for in the constitution. The election shall take place not earlier than three months nor later than six months after the proclamation by the Governor-General ordering such election. When the election of the officers provided for under the constitution has been held and the results determined, the Governor-General of the Philippine Islands shall certify the results of the election to the President of the United States, who shall thereupon issue a proclamation announcing the results of the election, and upon the issuance of such proclamation by the President the existing Philippine Government shall terminate and the new government shall enter upon its rights, privileges, powers, and duties, as provided under the constitution. The present Government of the Philippine Islands shall provide for the orderly transfer of the functions of government.

If a majority of the votes cast are against the constitution, the existing Government of the Philippine Islands shall continue without regard to the provisions of this Act.

Transfer of Property and Rights to Philippine Commonwealth

Section 5. All the property and rights which may have been acquired in the Philippine Islands by the United States under the treaties mentioned in the first section of this Act, except such land or other property as has heretofore been designated by the President of the United States for and other reservations of the Government of the United States, and except such land or other property or rights or interests therein as may have been sold or otherwise disposed of in accordance with law, are hereby granted to the government of the Commonwealth of the Philippine Islands when constituted.

Relations with the United States Pending Complete Independence

Section 6. After the date of the inauguration of the government of the Commonwealth of the Philippine Islands trade relations between the United States and the Philippine Islands shall be as now provided by law, subject to the following exceptions:

1. There shall be levied, collected, and paid on all refined sugars in excess of fifty thousand long tons, and on unrefined sugars in excess of eight hundred thousand long tons, coming into the United States from the Philippine Islands in any calendar year, the same rates of duty which are required by the laws of the United States to be levied, collected, and paid upon like articles imported from foreign countries.

2. There shall be levied, collected, and paid on all coconut oil coming into the United States from the Philippine Islands in any calendar year in excess of two hundred thousand long tons, the same rates of duty which are required by the laws of the United States to be levied, collected, and paid upon like articles imported from foreign countries.

3. There shall be levied, collected, and paid on all yarn, twine, cord, cordage, rope and cable, tarred or untarred, wholly or in chief value of Manila (abaca) or other hard fibers, coming into the United States from the Philippine Islands in any calendar year in excess of a collective total of three million pounds of all such articles hereinbefore enumerated, the same rates of duty which are required by the laws of the United States to be levied, collected, and paid upon like articles imported from foreign countries.

4. In the event that in any year the limit in the case of any article which may be exported to the United States free of duty shall be reached by the Philippine Islands, the amount or quantity of such articles produced or manufactured in the Philippine Islands thereafter that may be so exported to the United States free of duty shall be allocated, under export permits issued by the government of the Commonwealth of the Philippine Islands, to the producers or manufacturers of such articles proportionately on the basis of their exportation to the United States in the preceding year; except that in the case of unrefined sugar the amount thereof to be exported annually to the United States free of duty shall be allocated to the sugar-producing mills of the Islands proportionately on the basis

of their average annual production for the calendar years 1931, 1932, and 1933, and the amount of sugar from each mill which may be so exported shall be allocated in each year between the mill and the planters on the basis of the proportion of sugar to which the mill and the planters are respectively entitled. The Government of the Philippine Islands is authorized to adopt the necessary laws and regulations for putting into effect the allocation hereinbefore provided.

The government of the Commonwealth of the Philippine Islands shall impose and collect an export tax on all articles that may be exported to the United States from the articles that may be exported to the United States from the Philippine Islands free of duty under the provisions of existing law as modified by the foregoing provisions of this section including the articles enumerated in subdivisions (a), (b) and (c), within the limitations therein specified, as follows:

1. During the sixth year after the inauguration of the new government the export tax shall be 5 per centum of the rates of duty which are required by the laws of the United States to be levied, collected, and paid on like articles imported from foreign countries;
2. During the seventh year after the inauguration of the new government the export tax shall be 10 per centum of the rates of duty which are required by the laws of the United States to be levied, collected, and paid on like articles imported from foreign countries;
3. During the eighth year after the inauguration of the new government the export tax shall be 15 per centum of the rates of duty which are required by the laws of the United States to be levied, collected, and paid on like articles imported from foreign countries;
4. During the ninth year after the inauguration of the new government the export tax shall be 20 per centum of the rates of duty which are required by the laws of the United States to be levied, collected, and paid on like articles imported from foreign countries;
5. After the expiration of the ninth year of the inauguration of the new government the export tax shall be 25 per centum of the rates of duty which are required by the laws of the United States to be levied collected and paid on like articles imported from foreign countries.

The government of the Commonwealth of the Philippine Islands shall place all funds received in such export taxes in a sinking fund, and such funds shall, in addition to other moneys available for the purpose, be applied solely to the payment of the principal interest on the bonded indebtedness of the Philippine Islands, provinces, municipalities, and instrumentalities until such indebtedness has been fully discharged.

When used in this section in a geographical sense, the term "United States" includes all Territories and possessions of the United States, except the Philippine Islands, the Virgin Islands, American Samoa, and the island of Guam.

Section 7. Until the final and complete withdrawal of American sovereignty over the Philippine Islands—

1. Every duly adopted amendment to the constitution of the government of the Commonwealth of the Philippine Islands shall be submitted to the President of the United States for approval. If the President approves the amendment or if the President fails to disapprove such amendment within six months from the time of its submission, the amendment shall take effect as a part of such constitution.
2. The President of the United States shall have authority to suspend the taking effect of or the operation of any law, contract, or executive order of the government of the Commonwealth of the Philippine Islands, which in his judgment will result in a failure of the government of the Commonwealth of the Philippine Islands to fulfill its contracts, or to meet its bonded indebtedness and interest thereon or to provide for its sinking funds, or which seems likely to impair the reserves for the protection of the currency of the Philippine Islands, or which in his judgment will violate international obligations of the United States.
3. The Chief Executive of the Commonwealth of the Philippine Islands shall make an annual report to the President and Congress of the United States of the proceedings and operations of the government of the Commonwealth of the Philippine Islands and shall make such other reports as the President or Congress may request.

The President shall appoint, by and with the advice and consent of the Senate, a United States High Commissioner to the government of the Commonwealth of the Philippine Islands who shall hold office at the pleasure of the President and until his successor is appointed and qualified. He shall be known as the United States High Commissioner to the Philippine Islands. He shall be the representative of the President of the United States in the Philippine Islands and shall be recognized as such by the government of the Commonwealth of the Philippine Islands, by the commanding officers of the military forces of the United States, and by all civil officials of the United States in the Philippine Islands. He shall have access to all records of the government or any subdivision thereof, and shall be furnished by the Chief Executive of the Commonwealth of the Philippine Islands with such information as he shall request.

If the government of the Commonwealth of the Philippine Islands fails to pay any of its bonded or other indebtedness or the interest thereon when due or to fulfill any of its contracts, the United States High Commissioner shall immediately report the facts to the President, who may thereupon direct the High Commissioner to take over the customs offices and administration of the same, administer the same, and apply such part of the revenue received therefrom as may be necessary for the payment of such overdue indebtedness or for the fulfillment of such contracts. The United States High Commissioner shall annually, and at such other times as the President may require, render an official report to the President and Congress of the United States. He shall perform such additional duties and functions as may be delegated to him from time to time by the President under the provisions of this Act.

The United States High Commissioner shall receive the same compensation as is now received by the Governor-General of the Philippine Islands, and shall have such staff and assistants as the President may deem advisable and as may be appropriated for by Congress, including a financial expert, who shall receive for submission to the High Commissioner a duplicate copy of the reports to the insular auditor. Appeals from decisions of the insular auditor may be taken to the President of the United States. The salaries and expenses of the High Commissioner and his staff and assistants shall be paid by the United States.

The first United States High Commissioner appointed under this Act shall take office upon the inauguration of the new government of the Commonwealth of the Philippine Islands.

1. The government of the Commonwealth of the Philippine Islands shall provide for the selection of a Resident Commissioner to the United States, and shall fix his term of office. He shall be the representative of the government of the Commonwealth of the Philippine Islands and shall be entitled to official recognition as such by all departments upon presentation to the President of credentials signed by the Chief Executive of said government. He shall have a seat in the House of Representatives of the United States, with the right of debate, but without the right of voting. His salary and expenses shall be fixed and paid by the Government of the Philippine Islands. Until a Resident Commissioner is selected and qualified under this section, existing law governing the appointment of

Resident Commissioners from the Philippine Islands shall continue in effect.

2. Review by the Supreme Court of the United States of cases from the Philippine Islands shall be as now provided by law; and such review shall also extend to all cases involving the constitution of the Commonwealth of the Philippine Islands.

Section 8.

(a) Effective upon the acceptance of this Act by concurrent resolution of the Philippine Legislature or by a convention called for that purpose, as provided in section 17:

1. For the purposes of the Immigration Act of 1917, the Immigration Act of 1924 [except section 13(c)], this section, and all other laws of the United States relating to the immigration, exclusion, or expulsion of aliens, citizens of the Philippine Islands who are not citizens of the United States shall be considered as if they were aliens. For such purposes the Philippine Islands shall be considered as a separate country and shall have for each fiscal year a quota of fifty. This paragraph shall not apply to a person coming or seeking to come to the Territory of Hawaii who does not apply for and secure an immigration or passport visa, but such immigration shall be determined by the Department of the Interior on the basis of the needs of industries in the Territory of Hawaii.

2. Citizens of the Philippine Islands who are not citizens of the United States shall not be admitted to the continental United States from the Territory of Hawaii (whether entering such territory before or after the effective date of this section) unless they belong to a class declared to be non-immigrants by section 3 of the Immigration Act of 1924 or to a class declared to be nonquota immigrants under the provisions of section 4 of such Act other than subdivision (c) thereof, or unless they were admitted to such territory under an immigration visa. The Secretary of Labor shall by regulations provide a method for such exclusion and for the admission of such excepted classes.

3. Any Foreign Service officer may be assigned to duty in the Philippine Islands, under a commission as a consular officer, for such period as may be necessary and under such regulations as the Secretary of State may prescribe, during which assignment such officer shall be considered as stationed in a foreign country; but his powers and duties shall be confined to the performance of such of the official acts and notarial and other services, which such officer might properly perform in respect to the administration of the im-

migration laws if assigned to a foreign country as a consular officer, as may be authorized by the Secretary of State.

1. For the purposes of sections 18 and 20 of the Immigration Act of 1917, as amended, the Philippine Islands shall be considered a foreign country.

(b) The provisions of this section are in addition to the provisions of the immigration laws now in force, and shall be enforced as part of such laws, and all the penal or other provisions of such laws not applicable, shall apply to and be enforced in connection with the provisions of this section. An alien, although admissible under the provisions of this section, shall not be admitted to the United States if he is excluded by any provision of the immigration laws other than this section, and an alien, although admissible under the provisions of the immigration laws other than this section, shall not be admitted to the United States if he is excluded by any provision of this section.

(c) Terms defined in the Immigration Act of 1924 shall, when used in this section, have the meaning assigned to such terms in the Act.

Section 9. There shall be no obligation on the part of the United States to meet the interest or principal of bonds and other obligations of the Government of the Philippine Islands or of the provincial and municipal governments thereof, hereafter issued during the continuance of United States sovereignty in the Philippine Islands: Provided, That such bonds and obligations hereafter issued shall not be exempt from taxation in the United States or by authority of the United States.

Recognition of Philippine Independence and Withdrawal of American Sovereignty

Section 10.

(a) On the 4th day of July immediately following the expiration of a period of ten years from the date of the inauguration of the new government under the constitution provided for in this Act the President of the United States shall by proclamation withdraw and surrender all right of possession, supervision, jurisdiction, control, or sovereignty then existing and exercised by the United States in and over the territory and people of the Philippine Islands, including all military and other reservations of the Government of the United States in the Philippines (except such naval reservations and fueling stations as are reserved under section 5), and, on behalf of the United States, shall recognize the independence of the Philippine Islands as a separate and self-governing nation and acknowledge the authority and control over the same of the government instituted by the people thereof, under the constitution then in force.

(b) The President of the United States is hereby authorized and empowered to enter into negotiations with the Government of the Philippine Islands, not later than two years after his proclamation recognizing the independence of the Philippine Islands, for the adjustment and settlement of all questions relating to naval reservations and fueling stations of the United States in the Philippine Islands, and pending such adjustment and settlement the matter of naval reservations and fueling stations shall remain in its present status.

Neutralization of Philippine Islands

Section 11. The President is requested, at the earliest practicable date, to enter into negotiations with foreign powers with a view to the conclusion of a treaty for the perpetual neutralization of the Philippine Islands, if and when the Philippine independence shall have been achieved.

Notification to Foreign Governments

Section 12. Upon the proclamation and recognition of the independence of the Philippine Islands, the President shall notify the governments with which the United States is in diplomatic correspondence thereof and invite said governments to recognize the independence of the Philippine Islands.

Tariff Duties after Independence

Section 13. After the Philippine Islands have become a free and independent nation there shall be levied, collected, and paid upon all articles coming into the United States from the Philippine Islands the rates of duty which are required to be levied, collected, and paid upon like articles imported from other foreign countries: Provided, That at least one year prior to the date fixed in this Act for the independence of the Philippine Islands, there shall be held a conference of representatives of the Government of the United States and the Government of the Commonwealth of the Philippine Islands, such representatives to be appointed by the President of the United States and the Chief Executive of the Commonwealth of the Philippine Islands, respectively, for the purpose of formulating recommendations as to future trade relations between the Government of the United States and the independent Government of the Philippine Islands, the time, place, and manner of holding such conference to be determined by the President of the United States; but nothing in this proviso shall be construed to modify or affect in any way any provision of this Act relating to the procedure leading up to Philippine independence or the date upon which the Philippine Islands shall become independent.

Immigration after Independence

Section 14. Upon the final and complete withdrawal of American sovereignty over the Philippine Islands the immigration laws of the United States (including all the provisions thereof relating to persons ineligible to citizenship) shall apply to persons who were born in the Philippine Islands to the same extent as in the case of other foreign countries.

Certain Statutes Continued in Force

Section 15. Except as in this Act otherwise provided, the laws now or hereafter in force in the Philippine Islands shall continue in force in the Commonwealth of the Philippine Islands until altered, amended, or repealed by the Legislature of the Commonwealth of the Philippine Islands or by the Congress of the United States, and all references in such laws to the government or officials of the Philippines or Philippine Islands shall be construed, insofar as applicable, to refer to the government and corresponding officials respectively of the Commonwealth of the Philippine Islands. The government of the Commonwealth of the Philippine Islands shall be deemed successor to the present Government of the Philippine Islands and of all the rights and obligations thereof. Except as otherwise provided in this Act, all laws or parts of laws relating to the present Government of the Philippine Islands and its administration are hereby repealed as of the date of the inauguration of the government of the Commonwealth of the Philippine Islands.

Section 16. If any provision of this Act is declared unconstitutional or the applicability thereof to any person or circumstance is held invalid, the validity of the remainder of the Act and the applicability of such provisions to other persons and circumstances shall not be affected thereby.

Effective Date

Section 17. The foregoing provisions of this Act shall not take effect until accepted by concurrent resolution of the Philippine Legislature or by a convention called for the purpose of passing upon that question as may be provided by the Philippine Legislature.

Approved: March 24, 1934.

CROSS-STRAITS ECONOMIC COOPERATION FRAMEWORK AGREEMENT, JUNE 29, 2010

Preamble

The Straits Exchange Foundation and the Association for Relations Across the Taiwan Straits, adhering to the principles of equality, reciprocity and progressiveness and with a view to strengthening cross-Straits trade and economic relations,

Have agreed, in line with the basic principles of the World Trade Organization (WTO) and in consideration of the economic conditions of the two Parties, to gradually reduce or eliminate barriers to trade and investment for each other, create a fair trade and investment environment, further advance cross-Straits trade and investment relations by signing the *Cross-Straits Economic Cooperation Framework Agreement* (hereinafter referred to as this Agreement), and establish a cooperation mechanism beneficial to economic prosperity and development across the Straits.

The two Parties have agreed through consultations to the following:

Chapter 1. General Principles

Article 1. Objectives

The objectives of this Agreement are:

1. To strengthen and advance the economic, trade and investment cooperation between the two Parties;
2. To promote further liberalization of trade in goods and services between the two Parties and gradually establish fair, transparent and facilitative investment and investment protection mechanisms;
3. To expand areas of economic cooperation and establish a cooperation mechanism.

Article 2. Cooperation Measures

The two Parties have agreed, in consideration of their economic conditions, to take measures including but not limited to the following, in order to strengthen cross-Straits economic exchange and cooperation:

1. Gradually reducing or eliminating tariff and non-tariff barriers to trade in a substantial majority of goods between the two Parties;

2. Gradually reducing or eliminating restrictions on a large number of sectors in trade in services between the two Parties;
3. Providing investment protection and promoting two-way investment;
4. Promoting trade and investment facilitation and industry exchanges and cooperation.

Chapter 2. Trade and Investment

Article 3. Trade in Goods

1. The two Parties have agreed, on the basis of the Early Harvest for Trade in Goods as stipulated in Article 7 of this Agreement, to conduct consultations on an agreement on trade in goods no later than six months after the entry into force of this Agreement, and expeditiously conclude such consultations.

The consultations on the agreement on trade in goods shall include, but not be limited to:

1. modalities for tariff reduction or elimination;
2. rules of origin;
3. customs procedures;
4. non-tariff measures, including but not limited to technical barriers to trade (TBT) and sanitary and phytosanitary (SPS) measures;
5. trade remedy measures, including measures set forth in the *Agreement on Implementation of Article VI of the General Agreement on Tariffs and Trade 1994*, the *Agreement on Subsidies and Countervailing Measures* and the *Agreement on Safeguards* of the World Trade Organization, and the safeguard measures between the two Parties applicable to the trade in goods between the two Parties.

1. Goods included in the agreement on trade in goods pursuant to this Article shall be divided into three categories: goods subject to immediate tariff elimination, goods subject to phased tariff reduction, and exceptions or others.
2. Either Party may accelerate the implementation of tariff reduction at its discretion on the basis of the commitments to tariff concessions in the agreement on trade in goods.

Article 4. Trade in Services

1. The two Parties have agreed, on the basis of the Early Harvest for
   Trade in Services as stipulated in Article 8, to conduct consultations on an agreement on trade in services no later than six months
   after the entry into force of this Agreement, and expeditiously conclude such consultations.

The consultations on the agreement on trade in services shall seek to:

1. gradually reduce or eliminate restrictions on a large number of
   sectors in trade in services between the two Parties;
2. further increase the breadth and depth of trade in services;
3. enhance cooperation in trade in services between the two Parties.

1. Either Party may accelerate the liberalization or elimination of restrictive measures at its discretion on the basis of the commitments
   to liberalization in the agreement on trade in services.

Article 5. Investment

1. The two Parties have agreed to conduct consultations on the matters referred to in paragraph 2 of this Article within six months
   after the entry into force of this Agreement, and expeditiously
   reach an agreement.

Such an agreement shall include, but not be limited to, the following:

1. establishing an investment protection mechanism;
2. increasing transparency on investment-related regulations;
3. gradually reducing restrictions on mutual investments between
   the two Parties;
4. promoting investment facilitation.

Chapter 3. Economic Cooperation

Article 6. Economic Cooperation

To enhance and expand the benefits of this Agreement, the two Parties have agreed to strengthen cooperation in areas including, but not limited to, the following:

1. intellectual property rights protection and cooperation;
2. financial cooperation;
3. trade promotion and facilitation;
4. customs cooperation;
5. e-commerce cooperation;
6. discussion on the overall arrangements and key areas for industrial cooperation, promotion of cooperation in major projects, and coordination of the resolution of issues that may arise in the course of industrial cooperation between the two Parties;
7. promotion of small and medium-sized enterprises cooperation between the two Parties, and enhancement of the competitiveness of these enterprises;
8. promotion of the mutual establishment of offices by economic and trade bodies of the two Parties.

1. The two Parties shall expeditiously conduct consultations on the specific programs and contents of the cooperation matters listed in this Article.

Chapter 4. Early Harvest

Article 7. Early Harvest for Trade in Goods

1. To accelerate the realization of the objectives of this Agreement, the two Parties have agreed to implement the Early Harvest Program with respect to the goods listed in Annex I. The Early Harvest Program shall start to be implemented within six months after the entry into force of this Agreement.

The Early Harvest Program for trade in goods shall be implemented in accordance with the following rules:

1. The two Parties shall implement the tariff reductions in accordance with the product list and tariff reduction arrangements under the

Early Harvest stipulated in Annex I, unless their respective non-interim tariff rates generally applied on imports from all other WTO members are lower, in which case such rates shall apply;

2. The products listed in Annex I of this Agreement shall be subject to the Provisional Rules of Origin stipulated in Annex II. Each Party shall accord preferential tariff treatment to the above-mentioned products that are determined, pursuant to such Rules, as originating in the other Party upon importation;

3. The provisional trade remedy measures applicable to the products listed in Annex I of this Agreement refer to measures provided for in subparagraph (5) of paragraph 2 of Article 3 of this Agreement. The safeguard measures between the two Parties are specified in Annex III of this Agreement.

1. As of the date of the entry into force of the agreement on trade in goods to be reached by the two Parties pursuant to Article 3 of this Agreement, the Provisional Rules of Origin stipulated in Annex II and the provisional trade remedy measures provided for in subparagraph (3) of paragraph 2 of this Article shall cease to apply.

Article 8. Early Harvest for Trade in Services

1. To accelerate the realization of the objectives of this Agreement, the two Parties have agreed to implement the Early Harvest Program on the sectors and liberalization measures listed in Annex IV. The Early Harvest Program shall be implemented expeditiously after the entry into force of this Agreement.

The Early Harvest Program for Trade in Services shall be implemented in accordance with the following rules:

1. Each Party shall, in accordance with the Sectors and Liberalization Measures Under the Early Harvest for Trade in Services in Annex IV, reduce or eliminate the restrictive measures in force affecting the services and service suppliers of the other Party;

2. The definition of service suppliers stipulated in Annex V applies to the sectors and liberalization measures with respect to trade in services in Annex IV of this Agreement;

3. As of the date of the entry into force of the agreement on trade in services to be reached by the two Parties pursuant to Article 4 of this Agreement, the definitions of service suppliers stipulated in Annex V of this Agreement shall cease to apply;

4. In the event that the implementation of the Early Harvest Program for Trade in Services has caused a material adverse impact on the services sectors of one Party, the affected Party may request consultations with the other Party to seek a solution.

Chapter 5. Other Provisions

Article 9. Exceptions

No provision in this Agreement shall be interpreted to prevent either Party from adopting or maintaining exception measures consistent with the rules of the World Trade Organization.

Article 10. Dispute Settlement

1. The two Parties shall engage in consultations on the establishment of appropriate dispute settlement procedures no later than six months after the entry into force of this Agreement, and expeditiously reach an agreement in order to settle any dispute arising from the interpretation, implementation and application of this Agreement.
2. Any dispute over the interpretation, implementation and application of this Agreement prior to the date the dispute settlement agreement mentioned in paragraph 1 of this Article enters into force shall be resolved through consultations by the two Parties or in an appropriate manner by the Cross-Straits Economic Cooperation Committee to be established in accordance with Article 11 of this Agreement.

Article 11. Institutional Arrangements

The two Parties shall establish a Cross-Straits Economic Cooperation Committee (hereinafter referred to as the Committee), which consists of representatives designated by the two Parties. The Committee shall be responsible for handling matters relating to this Agreement, including but not limited to:

1. concluding consultations necessary for the attainment of the objectives of this Agreement;
2. monitoring and evaluating the implementation of this Agreement;
3. interpreting the provisions of this Agreement;
4. notifying important economic and trade information;

5. settling any dispute over the interpretation, implementation and application of this Agreement in accordance with Article 10 of this Agreement.

1. The Committee may set up working group(s) as needed to handle matters in specific areas pertaining to this Agreement, under the supervision of the Committee.
2. The Committee will convene a regular meeting on a semi-annual basis and may call *ad hoc* meeting(s) when necessary with consent of the two Parties.
3. Matters related to this Agreement shall be communicated through contact persons designated by the competent authorities of the two Parties.

Article 12. Documentation Formats

The two Parties shall use the agreed documentation formats for communication of matters arising from this Agreement.

Article 13. Annexes and Subsequent Agreements

All annexes to this Agreement and subsequent agreements signed in accordance with this Agreement shall be parts of this Agreement.

Article 14. Amendments

Amendments to this Agreement shall be subject to consent through consultations between, and confirmation in writing by, the two Parties.

Article 15. Entry into Force

After the signing of this Agreement, the two Parties shall complete the relevant procedures respectively and notify each other in writing. This Agreement shall enter into force as of the day following the date that both Parties have received such notification from each other.

Article 16. Termination

1. The Party terminating this Agreement shall notify the other Party in writing. The two Parties shall start consultations within 30 days from the date the termination notice is issued. In case the consultations fail to reach a consensus, this Agreement shall be terminated on the 180th day from the date the termination notice is issued by the notifying Party.

2. Within 30 days from the date of termination of this Agreement, the two Parties shall engage in consultations on issues arising from the termination.

This Agreement is signed in quadruplicate on this 29th day of June [2010] with each Party retaining two copies. The different wording of the corresponding text of this Agreement shall carry the same meaning, and all four copies are equally authentic.

- Annex I: Product List and Tariff Reduction Arrangements under the Early Harvest for Trade in Goods
- Annex II: Provisional Rules of Origin Applicable to Products under the Early Harvest for Trade in Goods
- Annex III: Safeguard Measures between the Two Parties Applicable to Products under the Early Harvest for Trade in Goods
- Annex IV: Sectors and Liberalization Measures under the Early Harvest for Trade in Services
- Annex V: Definitions of Service Suppliers Applicable to Sectors and Liberalization Measures under the Early Harvest for Trade in Services

Chairman President
Straits Exchange Foundation Association for Relations across the Taiwan Straits

CHARTER OF THE ASSOCIATION OF SOUTHEAST ASIAN NATIONS, 2007

Preamble

WE, THE PEOPLES of the Member States of the Association of Southeast Asian Nations (ASEAN), as represented by the Heads of State or Government of Brunei Darussalam, the Kingdom of Cambodia, the Republic of Indonesia, the Lao People's Democratic Republic, Malaysia, the Union of Myanmar, the Republic of the Philippines, the Republic of Singapore, the Kingdom of Thailand and the Socialist Republic of Viet Nam:
NOTING with satisfaction the significant achievements and expansion of ASEAN since its establishment in Bangkok through the promulgation of The ASEAN Declaration;
RECALLING the decisions to establish an ASEAN Charter in the Vientiane Action Programme, the Kuala Lumpur Declaration on the Establishment of the ASEAN Charter and the Cebu Declaration on the Blueprint of the ASEAN Charter;

MINDFUL of the existence of mutual interests and interdependence among the peoples and Member States of ASEAN which are bound by geography, common objectives and shared destiny;

INSPIRED by and united under One Vision, One Identity and One Caring and Sharing Community;

UNITED by a common desire and collective will to live in a region of lasting peace, security and stability, sustained economic growth, shared prosperity and social progress, and to promote our vital interests, ideals and aspirations;

RESPECTING the fundamental importance of amity and cooperation, and the principles of sovereignty, equality, territorial integrity, non-interference, consensus and unity in diversity;

ADHERING to the principles of democracy, the rule of law and good governance, respect for and protection of human rights and fundamental freedoms;

RESOLVED to ensure sustainable development for the benefit of present and future generations and to place the well-being, livelihood and welfare of the peoples at the centre of the ASEAN community building process;

CONVINCED of the need to strengthen existing bonds of regional solidarity to realise an ASEAN Community that is politically cohesive, economically integrated and socially responsible in order to effectively respond to current and future challenges and opportunities;

COMMITTED to intensifying community building through enhanced regional cooperation and integration, in particular by establishing an ASEAN Community comprising the ASEAN Security Community, the ASEAN Economic Community and the ASEAN Socio-Cultural Community, as provided for in the Bali Declaration of ASEAN Concord II;

HEREBY DECIDE to establish, through this Charter, the legal and institutional framework for ASEAN,

AND TO THIS END, the Heads of State or Government of the Member States of ASEAN, assembled in Singapore on the historic occasion of the 40th anniversary of the founding of ASEAN, have agreed to this Charter.

Chapter 1: Purposes and Principles

Article 1: Purposes

The Purposes of ASEAN are:

To maintain and enhance peace, security and stability and further strengthen peace-oriented values in the region;

To enhance regional resilience by promoting greater political, security, economic and socio-cultural cooperation;

To preserve Southeast Asia as a Nuclear Weapon-Free Zone and free of all other weapons of mass destruction;

To ensure that the peoples and Member States of ASEAN live in peace with the world at large in a just, democratic and harmonious environment;

To create a single market and production base which is stable, prosperous, highly competitive and economically integrated with effective facilitation for trade and investment in which there is free flow of goods, services and investment; facilitated movement of business persons, professionals, talents and labour; and freer flow of capital;

To alleviate poverty and narrow the development gap within ASEAN through mutual assistance and cooperation;

To strengthen democracy, enhance good governance and the rule of law, and to promote and protect human rights and fundamental freedoms, with due regard to the rights and responsibilities of the Member States of ASEAN;

To respond effectively, in accordance with the principle of comprehensive security, to all forms of threats, transnational crimes and trans-boundary challenges;

To promote sustainable development so as to ensure the protection of the region's environment, the sustainability of its natural resources, the preservation of its cultural heritage and the high quality of life of its peoples;

To develop human resources through closer cooperation in education and life-long learning, and in science and technology, for the empowerment of the peoples of ASEAN and for the strengthening of the ASEAN Community;

To enhance the well-being and livelihood of the peoples of ASEAN by providing them with equitable access to opportunities for human development, social welfare and justice;

To strengthen cooperation in building a safe, secure and drug-free environment for the peoples of ASEAN;

To promote a people-oriented ASEAN in which all sectors of society are encouraged to participate in, and benefit from, the process of ASEAN integration and community building;

To promote an ASEAN identity through the fostering of greater awareness of the diverse culture and heritage of the region; and

To maintain the centrality and proactive role of ASEAN as the primary driving force in its relations and cooperation with its external partners in a regional architecture that is open, transparent and inclusive.

Article 2: Principles

1. In pursuit of the Purposes stated in Article 1, ASEAN and its Member States reaffirm and adhere to the fundamental principles con-

tained in the declarations, agreements, conventions, concords, treaties and other instruments of ASEAN.

ASEAN and its Member States shall act in accordance with the following Principles:

1. respect for the independence, sovereignty, equality, territorial integrity and national identity of all ASEAN Member States;
2. shared commitment and collective responsibility in enhancing regional peace, security and prosperity;
3. renunciation of aggression and of the threat or use of force or other actions in any manner inconsistent with international law;
4. reliance on peaceful settlement of disputes;
5. non-interference in the internal affairs of ASEAN Member States;
6. respect for the right of every Member State to lead its national existence free from external interference, subversion and coercion;
7. enhanced consultations on matters seriously affecting the common interest of ASEAN;
8. adherence to the rule of law, good governance, the principles of democracy and constitutional government;
9. respect for fundamental freedoms, the promotion and protection of human rights, and the promotion of social justice;
10. upholding the United Nations Charter and international law, including international humanitarian law, subscribed to by ASEAN Member States;
11. abstention from participation in any policy or activity, including the use of its territory, pursued by any ASEAN Member State or non-ASEAN State or any non-State actor, which threatens the sovereignty, territorial integrity or political and economic stability of ASEAN Member States;
12. respect for the different cultures, languages and religions of the peoples of ASEAN, while emphasising their common values in the spirit of unity in diversity;
13. the centrality of ASEAN in external political, economic, social and cultural relations while remaining actively engaged, outward-looking, inclusive and non-discriminatory; and
14. adherence to multilateral trade rules and ASEAN's rules-based regimes for effective implementation of economic commitments and progressive reduction towards elimination of all barriers to regional economic integration, in a market-driven economy.

Chapter 2: Legal Personality

Article 3: Legal Personality of ASEAN

ASEAN, as an inter-governmental organisation, is hereby conferred legal personality.

Chapter 3: Membership

Article 4: Member States

The Member States of ASEAN are Brunei Darussalam, the Kingdom of Cambodia, the Republic of Indonesia, the Lao People's Democratic Republic, Malaysia, the Union of Myanmar, the Republic of the Philippines, the Republic of Singapore, the Kingdom of Thailand and the Socialist Republic of Viet Nam.

Article 5: Rights and Obligations

1. Member States shall have equal rights and obligations under this Charter.
2. Member States shall take all necessary measures, including the enactment of appropriate domestic legislation, to effectively implement the provisions of this Charter and to comply with all obligations of membership.
3. In the case of a serious breach of the Charter or noncompliance, the matter shall be referred to Article 20.

Article 6: Admission of New Members

1. The procedure for application and admission to ASEAN shall be prescribed by the ASEAN Coordinating Council.

Admission shall be based on the following criteria:

1. location in the recognised geographical region of Southeast Asia;
2. recognition by all ASEAN Member States;
3. agreement to be bound and to abide by the Charter; and
4. ability and willingness to carry out the obligations of Membership.

1. Admission shall be decided by consensus by the ASEAN Summit, upon the recommendation of the ASEAN Coordinating Council.
2. An applicant State shall be admitted to ASEAN upon signing an Instrument of Accession to the Charter.

Chapter 4: Organs

Article 7: ASEAN Summit

1. The ASEAN Summit shall comprise the Heads of State or Government of the Member States.

The ASEAN Summit shall:

1. be the supreme policy-making body of ASEAN;
2. deliberate, provide policy guidance and take decisions on key issues pertaining to the realization of the objectives of ASEAN, important matters of interest to Member States and all issues referred to it by the ASEAN Coordinating Council, the ASEAN Community Councils and ASEAN Sectoral Ministerial Bodies;
3. instruct the relevant Ministers in each of the Councils concerned to hold ad hoc inter-Ministerial meetings, and address important issues concerning ASEAN that cut across the Community Councils. Rules of procedure for such meetings shall be adopted by the ASEAN Coordinating Council;
4. address emergency situations affecting ASEAN by taking appropriate actions;
5. decide on matters referred to it under Chapters VII and VIII;
6. authorise the establishment and the dissolution of Sectoral Ministerial Bodies and other ASEAN institutions; and
7. appoint the Secretary-General of ASEAN, with the rank and status of Minister, who will serve with the confidence and at the pleasure of the Heads of State or Government upon the recommendation of the ASEAN Foreign Ministers Meeting.

ASEAN Summit Meetings shall be:

1. held twice annually, and be hosted by the Member State holding the ASEAN Chairmanship; and
2. convened, whenever necessary, as special or ad hoc meetings to be chaired by the Member State holding the ASEAN Chairmanship, at venues to be agreed upon by ASEAN Member States.

Article 8: ASEAN Coordinating Council

1. The ASEAN Coordinating Council shall comprise the ASEAN Foreign Ministers and meet at least twice a year.

The ASEAN Coordinating Council shall:

1. prepare the meetings of the ASEAN Summit;
2. coordinate the implementation of agreements and decisions of the ASEAN Summit;
3. coordinate with the ASEAN Community Councils to enhance policy coherence, efficiency and cooperation among them;
4. coordinate the reports of the ASEAN Community Councils to the ASEAN Summit;
5. consider the annual report of the Secretary-General on the work of ASEAN;
6. consider the report of the Secretary-General on the functions and operations of the ASEAN Secretariat and other relevant bodies;
7. approve the appointment and termination of the Deputy Secretaries-General upon the recommendation of the Secretary-General; and
8. undertake other tasks provided for in this Charter or such other functions as may be assigned by the ASEAN Summit.

1. The ASEAN Coordinating Council shall be supported by the relevant senior officials.

Article 9: ASEAN Community Councils

1. The ASEAN Community Councils shall comprise the ASEAN Political-Security Community Council, ASEAN Economic Community Council, and ASEAN Socio-Cultural Community Council.
2. Each ASEAN Community Council shall have under its purview the relevant ASEAN Sectoral Ministerial Bodies.
3. Each Member State shall designate its national representation for each ASEAN Community Council meeting.

In order to realise the objectives of each of the three pillars of the ASEAN Community, each ASEAN Community Council shall:

1. ensure the implementation of the relevant decisions of the ASEAN Summit;
2. coordinate the work of the different sectors under its purview, and on issues which cut across the other Community Councils; and
3. submit reports and recommendations to the ASEAN Summit on matters under its purview.

1. Each ASEAN Community Council shall meet at least twice a year and shall be chaired by the appropriate Minister from the Member State holding the ASEAN Chairmanship.
2. Each ASEAN Community Council shall be supported by the relevant senior officials.

Article 10: ASEAN Sectoral Ministerial Bodies

ASEAN Sectoral Ministerial Bodies shall:

1. function in accordance with their respective established mandates;
2. implement the agreements and decisions of the ASEAN Summit under their respective purview;
3. strengthen cooperation in their respective fields in support of ASEAN integration and community building; and
4. submit reports and recommendations to their respective Community Councils.

1. Each ASEAN Sectoral Ministerial Body may have under its purview the relevant senior officials and subsidiary bodies to undertake its functions as contained in Annex 1. The Annex may be updated by the Secretary-General of ASEAN upon the recommendation of the Committee of Permanent Representatives without recourse to the provision on Amendments under this Charter.

Article 11: Secretary-General of ASEAN and ASEAN Secretariat

1. The Secretary-General of ASEAN shall be appointed by the ASEAN Summit for a non-renewable term of office of five years, selected from among nationals of the ASEAN Member States based on alphabetical rotation, with due consideration to integrity, capability and professional experience, and gender equality.

The Secretary-General shall:

1. carry out the duties and responsibilities of this high office in accordance with the provisions of this Charter and relevant ASEAN instruments, protocols and established practices;
2. facilitate and monitor progress in the implementation of ASEAN agreements and decisions, and submit an annual report on the work of ASEAN to the ASEAN Summit;

3. participate in meetings of the ASEAN Summit, the ASEAN Community Councils, the ASEAN Coordinating Council, and ASEAN Sectoral Ministerial Bodies and other relevant ASEAN meetings;
4. present the views of ASEAN and participate in meetings with external parties in accordance with approved policy guidelines and mandate given to the Secretary-General; and
5. recommend the appointment and termination of the Deputy Secretaries-General to the ASEAN Coordinating Council for approval.

1. The Secretary-General shall also be the Chief Administrative Officer of ASEAN.
2. The Secretary-General shall be assisted by four Deputy Secretaries-General with the rank and status of Deputy Ministers. The Deputy Secretaries-General shall be accountable to the Secretary-General in carrying out their functions.
3. The four Deputy Secretaries-General shall be of different nationalities from the Secretary-General and shall come from four different ASEAN Member States.

The four Deputy Secretaries-General shall comprise:

1. two Deputy Secretaries-General who will serve a non-renewable term of three years, selected from among nationals of the ASEAN Member States based on alphabetical rotation, with due consideration to integrity, qualifications, competence, experience and gender equality; and
2. two Deputy Secretaries-General who will serve a term of three years, which may be renewed for another three years. These two Deputy Secretaries General shall be openly recruited based on merit.

1. The ASEAN Secretariat shall comprise the Secretary General and such staff as may be required.

The Secretary-General and the staff shall:

1. uphold the highest standards of integrity, efficiency, and competence in the performance of their duties;
2. not seek or receive instructions from any government or external party outside of ASEAN; and

3. refrain from any action which might reflect on their position as ASEAN Secretariat officials responsible only to ASEAN.

1. Each ASEAN Member State undertakes to respect the exclusively ASEAN character of the responsibilities of the Secretary-General and the staff, and not to seek to influence them in the discharge of their responsibilities.

FRAMEWORK FOR COMPREHENSIVE ECONOMIC PARTNERSHIP BETWEEN THE ASSOCIATION OF SOUTHEAST ASIAN NATIONS AND JAPAN, OCTOBER 8, 2003

WE, the Heads of State/Governments of Brunei Darussalam, the Kingdom of Cambodia, the Republic of Indonesia, the Lao People's Democratic Republic ("Lao PDR"), Malaysia, the Union of Myanmar, the Republic of the Philippines, the Republic of Singapore, the Kingdom of Thailand and the Socialist Republic of Viet Nam, Member States of the Association of Southeast Asian Nations (collectively, "ASEAN" or "ASEAN Member States", or individually, "ASEAN Member State"), and Japan gathered today for the ASEAN–Japan Summit;

RECALLING the Joint Declaration made at the ASEAN–Japan Summit held on 5 November 2002 in Phnom Penh, Cambodia to implement measures for the realization of a Comprehensive Economic Partnership ("CEP"), including elements of a possible Free Trade Area ("FTA"), which should be completed as soon as possible within 10 years, and to establish a Committee to consider and draft a framework for the realization of the CEP between ASEAN and Japan ("ASEAN–Japan CEP");

INSPIRED by the significant progress made in ASEAN–Japan relations, which has spanned 30 years of an economic partnership that has been expanding over a wide range of areas;

DESIRING to minimize barriers and deepen economic linkages between ASEAN and Japan; lower business costs; increase intra-regional trade and investment; increase economic efficiency; create a larger market with greater opportunities and larger economies of scale for the businesses of both ASEAN and Japan; and enhance our attractiveness to capital and talent;

SHARING the view that the ASEAN–Japan CEP should benefit from and complementary to the economic integration of ASEAN and considering that achievement of the ASEAN Free Trade Area ("AFTA") will enhance the value of ASEAN as a regional market and attract investment to ASEAN and that it is desirable that the Common Effective Preferential Tariff ("CEPT") Scheme among ASEAN Member States be implemented on a timely basis;

BEING confident that the establishment of an ASEAN–Japan FTA covering trade in goods, services and investment will create a partnership between ASEAN and Japan, and provide an important mechanism for strengthening co-operation and supporting economic stability in East Asia;

RECOGNISING the important role and contribution of the business sector in enhancing trade and investment between ASEAN and Japan and the need to further promote and facilitate their co-operation and utilisation of greater business opportunities provided by the ASEAN–Japan CEP;

RECOGNISING the different stages of economic development among ASEAN Member States and between ASEAN and Japan, and the need to facilitate the increasing participation of the Kingdom of Cambodia, Lao PDR, the Union of Myanmar and the Socialist Republic of Viet Nam, (collectively, "the newer ASEAN Member States") in the ASEAN–Japan CEP;

REAFFIRMING the rights and obligations of the respective countries under the Marrakesh Agreement Establishing the World Trade Organization ("WTO Agreement"), and other multilateral, regional and bilateral agreements and arrangements;

RECOGNISING the catalytic role that regional trade arrangements can contribute towards accelerating regional and global liberalization and as building blocks in the framework of the multilateral trading system;

HAVE DECIDED AS FOLLOWS:

1. Objectives

The objectives of the ASEAN–Japan CEP are to:

1. Strengthen economic integration between ASEAN and Japan through the creation of a CEP;
2. Enhance the competitiveness of ASEAN and Japan in the world market through strengthened partnership and linkages;
3. Progressively liberalize and facilitate trade in goods and services as well as create a transparent and liberal investment regime;
4. Explore new areas and develop appropriate measures for further co-operation and economic integration; and
5. Facilitate the more effective economic integration of the newer ASEAN Member States and bridge the development gap among the ASEAN Member States.

2. Basic Principles

ASEAN and Japan will adhere to the following principles:

1. The ASEAN–Japan CEP should involve all ASEAN Member States and Japan and include a broad range of sectors focusing on liberalisation, facilitation and co-operation activities, noting the principle of reciprocity, transparency and mutual benefits to both ASEAN and Japan;
2. The integrity, solidarity and integration of ASEAN will be given consideration in the realisation of the ASEAN–Japan CEP;
3. The ASEAN–Japan CEP Agreement should be consistent with the rules and disciplines of the WTO Agreement;
4. Special and differential treatment should be provided to the ASEAN Member States in recognition of their different levels of economic development. Additional flexibility should be accorded to the newer ASEAN Member States;
5. Flexibility should be given to address the sensitive sectors in each ASEAN Member State and Japan; and
6. Technical co-operation and capacity building programmes should also be considered.

3. Measures for Comprehensive Economic Partnership

The ASEAN–Japan CEP should be realised by:

1. Carrying out the Measures for Immediate Implementation specified in Section 4;
2. Implementing programmes on Facilitation and Co-operation between ASEAN and Japan in the areas specified in Section 5; and
3. Implementing measures for Liberalisation in (1) trade in Goods; (2) trade in Services; and (3) investment.

4. Measures for Immediate Implementation

ASEAN and Japan decide to work on the following activities that could provide immediate benefits on an accelerated basis:

1. Technical assistance and capacity building to ASEAN, particularly for the newer ASEAN Member States, so as to improve their competitiveness to meaningfully participate in the partnership and to assist ASEAN Member States who are not members of WTO and World Customs Organization ("WCO") to work towards becoming members of the aforementioned organizations;

2. Trade and investment promotion and facilitation measures;
3. Trade and investment policy dialogue;
4. Business sector dialogue;
5. Measures to facilitate the mobility of business people;
6. Exchange and compilation of relevant data such as customs tariff and bilateral trade statistics; and
7. Any other measures delivering immediate mutual benefits.

1. ASEAN and Japan will continue to build upon existing or agreed programmes in the areas identified above.

5. Facilitation and Co-operation

ASEAN and Japan decide to conduct consultations from the beginning of 2004 on the areas of facilitation and co-operation, and to develop work programmes for the expeditious implementation of measures or activities in each of the following areas:

1. Trade Related Procedures. Facilitation of trade-related procedures will be implemented in such areas as cooperation on custom procedures by computerization, simplification and harmonization, as far as possible, to relevant international standards.
2. Business Environment. Recognizing that the satisfactory business environment is an indispensable part of the attractiveness to investors, each ASEAN Member State and Japan will make the effort to improve the business environment and enhance co-operation in related fields.
3. Intellectual Property Rights ("IPR"). Japan will support ASEAN Member States in developing, improving, enhancing and implementing their IPR capabilities, and in promoting accession to IPR-related international agreements. Co-operation between ASEAN and Japan, such as information exchange, will also be encouraged.

Other Areas of Co-operation:

- Energy. Co-operation in oil stockpiling, natural gas utilization and promotion of energy efficiency.
- Information and Communications Technology ("ICT"). Co-operation in developing ICT infrastructure, Information Technology ("IT")–related legal systems, and IT-related human resource, and promoting exchanges of IT researchers and engineers.

- Human Resource Development ("HRD"). Co-operation among the relevant organisations in each ASEAN Member State and Japan, especially in the field of HRD for experienced engineers and middle management.
- Small and Medium Enterprises ("SMEs"). Co-operation in exchanging views on policies relating to SMEs and expanding business opportunities of SMEs.
- Tourism and Hospitality. Co-operation in implementing seminars or information exchange on tourism and hospitality.
- Transportation and Logistics. Co-operation for efficient cargo transport system, safe and sustainable shipping and safe and efficient air transport.
- Standards and Conformance and Mutual Recognition Arrangement. Exchange of information concerning the standards and conformance policies, and capacity building of standardisation organisations in each ASEAN Member State.
- Other possible technical co-operation projects, including environment, automobile, biotechnology, science and technology, sustainable forest management, competition policy, food security and financial services co-operation.

1. ASEAN and Japan will continue to develop work programmes in new areas of facilitation and co-operation.

6. Liberalisation

1. ASEAN and Japan will start the consultations on the AS-EAN–Japan CEP on the liberalisation of trade in goods, trade in services, and investment, from the beginning of 2004 by discussing the basic principles of ASEAN–Japan cumulative rules of origin and customs classification and collecting and analyzing trade and custom data.
2. ASEAN and Japan will initiate a negotiation on the CEP Agreement between ASEAN and Japan as a whole, taking into account the achievements of bilateral negotiations between each ASEAN Member State and Japan, and the further progress of the ASEAN integration process. Such Agreement should be consistent with the WTO Agreement.
3. During the negotiation, those ASEAN Member States that have not concluded bilateral Economic Partnership Agreement ("EPA") with Japan will negotiate concessions bilaterally. Schedules of liberalization concessions between Japan and those ASEAN Member States that have concluded a bilateral EPA should not be renegotiated in the negotiation of the ASEAN–Japan CEP Agreement. All

schedules of liberalization concessions will be annexed to the AS-EAN–Japan CEP Agreement.

(1) Trade in Goods

ASEAN and Japan decide to progressively eliminate duties and other restrictive regulations of commerce, except, where necessary, those permitted under Article XXIV(8)(b) of the General Agreement on Tariffs and Trade 1994 in Annex 1A to the WTO Agreement ("GATT") on substantially all trade in goods in order to establish an FTA between ASEAN and Japan which will include, but will not be limited, to the following:

1. Cumulative rules of origin;
2. Detailed rules governing the tariff reduction or elimination programmes including principles governing reciprocal commitments;
3. Non-tariff measures including technical barriers to trade; and
4. Trade remedy measures based on the principles of the WTO Agreement.

(2) Trade in Services

ASEAN and Japan decide to progressively liberalize trade in services with substantial sectoral coverage consistent with the rules of the WTO Agreement. Such liberalizations should be directed to:

1. Progressive elimination of substantially all discrimination between or among ASEAN and Japan and/or prohibition of new or more discriminatory measures with respect to trade in services between ASEAN and Japan, (except for measures permitted under Article V(1)(b) of the General Agreement on Trade in Services ("GATS") in Annex 1B to the WTO Agreement);
2. Expansion in the depth and scope of liberalization of trade in services;
3. Facilitation of the entry and temporary movement of business people; and
4. Enhanced co-operation in services between ASEAN and Japan in order t o improve efficiency and competitiveness.

(3) Investment

In order to promote investment, ASEAN and Japan decide to:

1. Create a liberal and competitive environment;
2. Strengthen co-operation in investment, facilitate investment and improve transparency of investment rules and regulations; and

3. Provide for the protection of investors and investment.

Most-Favored-Nation Treatment

For ASEAN Member States which are not yet WTO members, Japan will continue to apply the general Most-Favored-Nation ("MFN") treatment as stipulated in Article I of GATT. Japan will endeavour to provide MFN treatment under the WTO on a reciprocal basis.

8. General Exceptions

Subject to the requirement that such measures are not applied in a manner which would constitute a means of arbitrary or unjustifiable discrimination between or among ASEAN and Japan where the same conditions prevail, or a disguised restriction on trade within the ASEAN–Japan CEP, nothing in this Framework should prevent any individual ASEAN Member State and/or Japan from adopting or enforcing measures, in accordance with the rules and disciplines of the WTO Agreement, for:

1. The protection of the national security of each ASEAN Member State and/or Japan;
2. The protection of articles of artistic, historic and archaeological value; or
3. Such other measures which each ASEAN Member State and/or Japan deems or deem necessary for the protection of public morals or to maintain public order, or for the protection of human, animal or plant life and health.

9. Consultation

Any differences concerning the interpretation or implementation of this Framework should be settled amicably by consultations and/or mediation.

10. Timeframes

1. ASEAN and Japan will start consultations on the ASEAN–Japan CEP on the liberalization of trade in goods, trade in services and investment, from the beginning of 2004, as set forth in Section 6, paragraph 1.
2. ASEAN and Japan will make maximum efforts to commence the negotiation on the CEP Agreement between ASEAN and Japan as a whole, referred to in Section 6, paragraph 2, from the beginning of 2005. ASEAN and Japan will endeavor to conclude the negotia-

tion as soon as possible, taking into account the need to leave sufficient time for implementation.

3. The implementation of measures for the realization of the ASEAN–Japan CEP, including elements of a possible free trade area, should be completed as soon as possible by 2012, taking into account the economic levels and sensitive sectors in each country, including allowing additional five (5) years' time for the newer ASEAN Member States.

11. Institutional Arrangements for this Framework

1. The ASEAN–Japan Committee on Comprehensive Economic Partnership ("AJCCEP") will continue to carry out the work set out in this Framework.
2. AJCCEP may establish other bodies as may be necessary to co-ordinate and implement this Framework, including the supervision, co-ordination and review of the implementation of other measures undertaken pursuant to this Framework.
3. The ASEAN Secretariat will provide the necessary secretariat support to the AJCCEP whenever and wherever the meetings are held. SIGNED on the Eighth Day of October in the year Two Thousand and Three in Bali, Indonesia, in duplicate in the English language.

Appendix D
Acronyms and Abbreviations

APEAC	Asia-Pacific Economic Cooperation
ASEAN	Association of Southeast Asian Nations
bbl	barrel
bcm	billion cubic meters
Comecon	Council for Mutual Economic Cooperation
CNOOC	Chinese National Offshore Oil Company
CNPC	Chinese National Petroleum Corporation
CPC	Chinese Petroleum Corporation
EEZ	exclusive economic zone
EIA	Energy Information Agency
FDI	foreign direct investment
GDP	gross domestic product
GSC	global service center
LNG	liquefied natural gas
LPG	liquefied petroleum gas
PLAN	People's Liberation Army Navy
PNOC	Philippine National Oil Company
PRC	People's Republic of China
RCEP	Regional Comprehensive Economic Partnership
SCS	South China Sea
Sinopec	China Petroleum and Chemical Corporation
SEZ	special economic zones
TPP	Trans-Pacific Partnership

| UN | United Nations |
| UNCLOS | United Nations Convention on the Law of the Sea |

Appendix E
South China Sea Maps

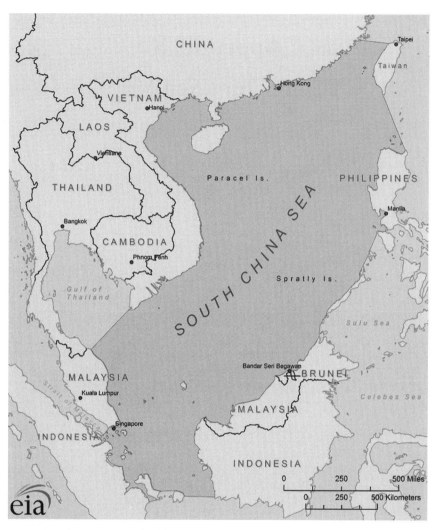

Map of the South China Sea. *eia*

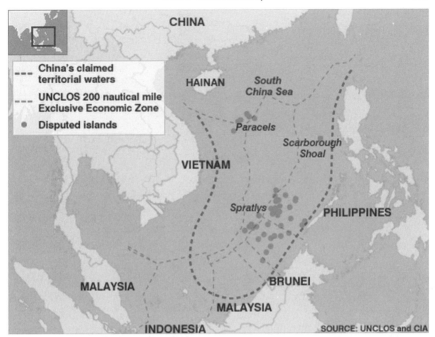

Map of China's Claims in the South China Sea and how they overlap with other nations. *UNCLOS and CIA*

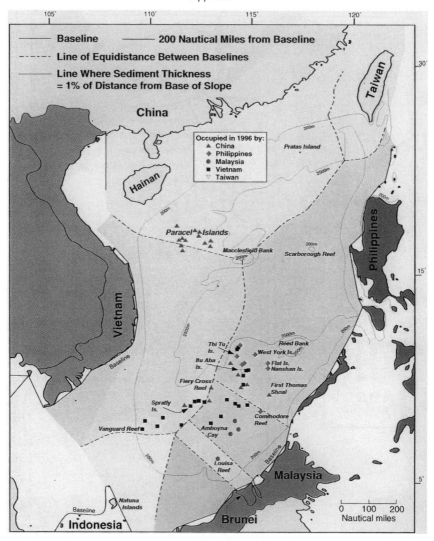

Map of South China Sea claims divided by distance from claimant nation's coast.

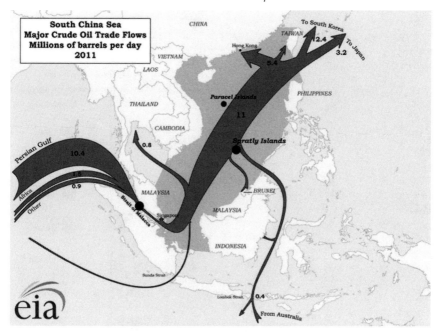

Oil flows through the South China Sea Region. *eia*

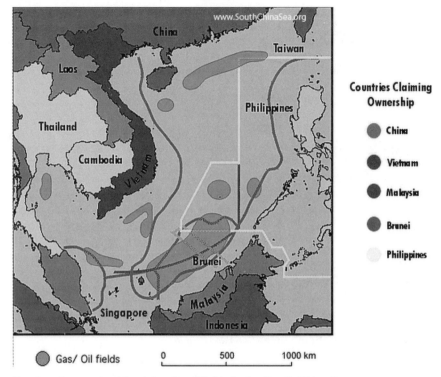

Countries Claiming Ownership

● China

● Vietnam

● Malaysia

● Brunei

● Philippines

● Gas/ Oil fields

0   500   1000 km

Overlapping ownership claims in oil fields in the South China Sea.
www.southchinasea.org

Bibliography

CHAPTER 1

Buszynski, Leszek. "The South China Sea: Oil, Maritime Claims, and U.S.–China Strategic Rivalry." *The Washington Quarterly* (Spring 2012), p. 140.
"A Country Study: Vietnam." *Library of Congress Country Studies* (March 22, 2011). [online] http://lcweb2.loc.gov/frd/cs/vntoc.html. Accessed March 24, 2013.
Gallagher, Michael G. "China's Illusory Threat to the South China Sea." *International Security*, vol. 19, no. 1 (Summer 1994), p. 171.
Hull, Richard E. "The South China Sea: Future Source of Prosperity or Conflict in South East Asia?" *National Defense University, Strategic Forum*, no. 60 (February 1996).
"The Island of Palmas Case." *Permanent Court of Arbitration* (April 4, 1928). [online] www.pca cpa.org/showfile.asp?fil_id=168. Accessed March 23, 2013.
Morton, Brian, and Grasham Blackmore. "South China Sea." *Marine Pollution Bulletin*, vol. 42, no. 12 (2001), p. 1236.
Page, Tom. "India, China Standoff with China over Sea Oil." *Wall Street Journal* (September 23, 2011). [online] http://online.wsj.com/article/SB10001424053111904563904576586620948411618.html. Accessed March 24, 2013.
Ring, Andrew. "A U.S. South China Sea Perspective: Just over the Horizon." *Weatherhead Center for International Affairs* (July 4, 2012). pp. 27–28.
Rosenberg, David. "Why a South China Sea Website." *The South China Sea* (2010). [online] http://www.southchinasea.org/why-a-south-china-sea-website-an-introductory-essay. Accessed May 31, 2013.
Storey, Ian James. "Creeping Assertiveness: China, the Philippines and the South China Sea Dispute." *Contemporary Southeast Asia*, vol. 21, no. 1 (April 1999). p. 96.
"United Nations Convention on the Law of the Sea of 10 December 1982." *United Nations Division of Ocean Affairs and Law of the Sea* (November 9, 2011). [Online] http://www.un.org/Depts/los/convention_agreements/convention_overview_convention.htm. Accessed March 24, 2013.
Watts, Alex. "Tensions Rise as Vietnam Accuses China of Sabotage." *Sydney Morning Herald* (June 2, 2011). [online] http://www.smh.com.au/world/tensions-rise-as-vietnam-accuseschina-of-sabotage-20110601-1fgno.html. Accessed May 31, 2013.
World Trade Organization. "Trade Patterns and Global Value Chains in East Asia: From Trade in Goods to Trade in Tasks." Geneva, Switzerland, 2011.

CHAPTER 2

"About PetroChina." *PetroChina Company Limited* (2008). [online] http://www.petrochina.com.cn/Ptr/About_PetroChina/Company_Profile/?COLLCC=589709553&. Accessed April 2, 2013.
"About Sinopec." *Sinopec Corp.* (2011). [online] http://english.sinopec.com/about_sinopec/our_company/6as7tuvr.shtml. Accessed April 2, 2013.
"About TNK-BP." *TNK-BP* (2013). [online] http://www.tnk-bp.com/en/company. Accessed March 31, 2013.

Central Intelligence Agency. "China." *World Factbook* (2013). [online] https://www.cia.gov/library/publications/the-world-factbook/geos/ch.html. Accessed, March 29, 2013.

———. "Malaysia." *World Factbook* (2013). [online] https://www.cia.gov/library/publications/the world-factbook/geos/my.html. Accessed, March 29, 2013.

———. "Philippines." *World Factbook* (2013). [online] https://www.cia.gov/library/publications/the world-factbook/geos/rp.html. Accessed March 29, 2013.

———. "Taiwan." *World Factbook* (2013). [online] https://www.cia.gov/library/publications/the world-factbook/geos/tw.html. Accessed, March 29, 2013.

———. "Vietnam." *World Factbook* (2013). [online] https://www.cia.gov/library/publications/the world-factbook/geos/vm.html. Accessed, March 29, 2013.

"A Country Study: Vietnam." *Library of Congress Country Studies* (March 22, 2011). [online] http://lcweb2.loc.gov/frd/cs/vntoc.html. Accessed, March 24, 2013.

Downs, Erica S. "Who's Afraid of China's Oil Companies?" In Jonathan Elkind and Carlos Pacual, eds. *Energy Security: Economics, Politics, Strategy, and Implications* (Washington, DC: Brookings Institute, 2010). [online] http://www.brookings.edu/~/media/research/files/papers/2010/7/china%20oil%20downs/07_china_oil_downs.pdf. Accessed June 1, 2013.

Hurst, Cindy. "China's Global Quest for Energy." *Institute for the Analysis of Global Security* (January 2007). [online] http://fmso.leavenworth.army.mil/documents/chinasquest0107.pdf. Accessed June 1, 2013.

Kon, Chong Pooi, and Barry Porter. "Petronas to Complete C 5.2 Billion Progress Deal This Week." *Bloomberg* (December 9, 2012). [online] http://www.bloomberg.com/news/2012-12-10/petronas-to-complete-c-5-2-billion-progress-deal-this-week-1-.html. Accessed March 29, 2013.

"Malaysia Oil and Gas Report Q3 2013." *Business Monitor International* (February 2013). pp. 9–21.

"Petronas' Annual Profit Down 17%." *Today* (March 7, 2013). [online] http://www.todayonline.com/business/petronas-annual-profit-down-17. Accessed March 30, 2013.

"Philippines Oil and Gas Report Q3 2013." *Business Monitor* (February 2013). p. 7.

"Profile: CNOOC Ltd. (0833.HK)." *Reuters* (n.d.). [online] http://in.reuters.com/finance/stocks/companyProfile?symbol=0883.HK. Accessed April 2, 2013.

"South China Sea." *U.S. Energy Information Agency* (February 7, 2013). p. 1. [online] http://www.eia.gov/countries/analysisbriefs/South_China_Sea/south_china_sea.pdf. Accessed June 1, 2013.

"Sudan: A Chronology of Key Events." *BBC News* (March 14, 2013). [online] http://www.bbc.co.uk/news/world-africa-14095300. Accessed March 25, 2013.

"Taiwan." *U.S. Energy Information Agency* (February 12, 2013). [online] http://www.eia.gov/countries/country data.cfm?fips=TW. Accessed March 31, 2013.

"Taiwan Oil and Gas Report Q3 2013." *Business Monitor* (February 2013). pp. 40–48.

"Vietnam Oil and Gas Report Q3 2013." *Business Monitor* (February 2013). pp. 55–68.

Watts, Alex. "Tensions Rise as Vietnam Accuses China of Sabotage." *Sydney Morning Herald* (June 2, 2011). [online] http://www.smh.com.au/world/tensions-rise-as-vietnam-accuseschina-of-sabotage-20110601-1fgno.html. Accessed May 31, 2013.

CHAPTER 3

"2012 Investment Climate Statement—Brunei." *U.S. Department of State* (June 2012). [online] http://www.state.gov/e/eb/rls/othr/ics/2012/191116.htm. Accessed April 5, 2013.

"2012 Investment Climate Statement—Taiwan." *U.S. Department of State* (June 2012). [online] http://www.state.gov/e/eb/rls/othr/ics/2012/191245.htm. Accessed April 7, 2013.

"As China Opens Its Doors, Coca-Cola Pours In: Trade: The Soft Drink Maker Is Building More Plants and Has Plans to Reach More of the Nation's Huge Market as Its Economy Strengthens," *Los Angeles Times* (November 8, 1993). [online] http://articles.latimes.com/1993-11-08/business/fi 54690_1_soft-drink. Accessed April 7, 2013.

Bakar, Al-Haadi Abu. "GE Opens Brunei Office." *Brunei Times* (July 1, 2012). [online] http://www.bt.com.bn/business-national/2012/07/01/ge-opens-brunei-office. Accessed April 1, 2013.

Brettman, Allan. "Nike Relies Even More on Vietnam for Shoes, Annual Report Shows." *The Oregonian* (July 25, 2012). [online] http://www.oregonlive.com/playbooks-profits/index.ssf/2012/07/nike_relies_even_more_on_vietn.html. Accessed April 5, 2013.

"Brunei Darussalam." *Office of the United States Trade Representative* (n.d.). [online] http://www.ustr.gov/countries-regions/southeast-asia-pacific/brunei-darussalam. Accessed April 4, 2013.

Burkitt, Laurie. "China Accuses Coca-Cola of Illegally Using GPS." *Wall Street Journal* (March 13, 2013). [online] http://online.wsj.com/article/SB10001424127887323826704578357131413767460.html. Accessed April 4, 2013.

Central Intelligence Agency. "Brunei." *World Factbook* (2013). [online] https://www.cia.gov/library/publications/the-world-factbook/geos/bx.html. Accessed April 3, 2012.

———. "China." *World Factbook* (2013). [online] https://www.cia.gov/library/publications/the-world-factbook/geos/bx.html. Accessed March 31, 2013.

———. "Indonesia." *World Factbook* (2013). [online] https://www.cia.gov/library/publications/the-world-factbook/geos/id.html. Accessed April 3, 2012.

———. "Malaysia." *World Factbook* (2013). [online] https://www.cia.gov/library/publications/the-world-factbook/geos/my.html. Accessed April 3, 2012.

———. "Philippines." *World Factbook* (2013). [online] https://www.cia.gov/library/publications/the-world-factbook/geos/rp.html. Accessed April 3, 2012.

———. "Taiwan." *World Factbook* (2013). [online] https://www.cia.gov/library/publications/the world-factbook/geos/tw.html. Accessed April 3, 2012.

———. "Vietnam." *World Factbook* (2013). [online] https://www.cia.gov/library/publications/the-world-factbook/geos/vm.html. Accessed April 3, 2012.

"Citi in the Philippines." *Citibank Philippines* (2012). [online] http://www.citibank.com.ph/gcb/footer/aboutus.htm. Accessed April 23, 2013.

"Coca-Cola Inaugurates US$160 Million Bottling Plant in China Creating 500 Direct Jobs; To Invest US$ 4 Billion over 3 Years." *FDI Tracker* (March 30, 2012). [online] http://www.fditracker.com/2012/03/coca-cola-inaugurates-us160-million.html. Accessed April 7, 2013.

Corning Incorporated. "A Day Made of Glass . . . Made Possible by Corning." *YouTube* (2011). [online] http://www.youtube.com/watch?v=6Cf7IL_eZ38. Accessed June 2, 2013.

"Delicious and Delightful New Year." *Coca-Cola History and Coke Memorabilia* (2010). [online] http://www.7xpub.com/coke-articles-and-essays/1625-delicious-and-delightful-new-year.html. Accessed April 5, 2013.

"Economic Update: The Philippines: BPO's Rising Potential." *Oxford Business Group* (April 24, 2012). [online] http://www.oxfordbusinessgroup.com/economic_updates/philippines-bpo%E2%80%99s-rising-potential. Accessed April 7, 2013.

"Gap Inc. Expands in Asia Pacific with First Stores in Vietnam and Guam." *Gap Inc.* (August 22, 2011). [online] http://www.gapinc.com/content/gapinc/html/media/pressrelease/2011/med_pr_VietnamGuam.html. Accessed April 7, 2013.

"Gap Inc.'s Global Runway." *Gap Inc.* (November 17, 2011). [online] http://www.gapinc.com/content/dam/gapincsite/documents/GPS_Global_Runway_Backgrounder.pdf. Accessed April 7, 2013.

Hieber, Murray, and Liam Hanlon. "ASEAN and Partners Launch Regional Comprehensive Economic Partnership." *Center for Strategic and Intelligence Studies* (December 7, 2012). [online] http://csis.org/publication/asean-and-partners-launch-regional-comprehensive-economic-partnership. Accessed April 1, 2013.

"History." *Asia-Pacific Economic Cooperation* (2013). [online] http://www.apec.org/About-Us/About-APEC/History.aspx. Accessed April 3, 2013.

"History." *Association of Southeast Asian Nations* (2012). [online] http://www.asean.org/asean/about-asean/history. Accessed March 30, 2013.

"Introduction to the Enterprises." *Taiwan Free Trade Zone* (2011). [online] http://taiwanftz.com/lp.asp?ctNode=542&ctUnit=206&baseDSD=52&mp=3. Accessed April 7, 2013.

"Investment." *U.S. TaiwanConnect* (2013). [online] www.ustaiwanconnect.org/US-Taiwan-Relations/Investment. Accessed April 5, 2013.

Ismail, Fauziah. "U.S. Companies Ready to Pump More Money into Malaysia." *New Strait Times* (May 19, 2012). [online] http://www.nst.com.my/top-news/us-companies-ready-to-pump-more-money-into-malaysia 1.85573. Accessed April 5, 2013.

Mah, Randal. "Procter and Gamble Takes 100 Million Indonesia Plunge." *Emerging Money* (October 5, 2011). [online] http://emergingmoney.com/consumer/procter-gamble-takes-100-million-indonesia-plunge. Accessed February 12, 2013.

"Malaysia Oil and Gas Report Q3 2013." *Business Monitor International* (February 2013). pp. 9–21.

"Microsoft Technology Center: Taipei." *Microsoft* (2013). [online] http://www.microsoft.com/en-us/mtc/locations/taipei.aspx. Accessed April 7, 2013.

"Our Mission: To Bring Inspiration and Innovation to Every Athlete in the World." *Nike, Inc.* (2013). [online] http://nikeinc.com/pages/about-nike-inc. Accessed April 2, 2013.

"The People's Republic of China." *Office of the United States Trade Representative* (n.d.). [online] http://www.ustr.gov/countries-regions/china-mongolia-taiwan/peoples-republic-china. Accessed April 2, 2013.

Perlez, Jane. "Asian Nations Plan Trade Bloc That, Unlike U.S.'s, Invites China." *New York Times* (November 20, 2012). [online] http://www.nytimes.com/2012/11/21/world/asia/southeast-asian-nations-announce-trade-bloc-to-rival-us-effort.html. Accessed April 7, 2013.

"Philippines." *J.P.Morgan* (2013). [online] http://www.jpmorgan.com/pages/jpmorgan/ap/philippines. Accessed April 3, 2013.

"PM U.S. Companies to Invest Billion in the Country." *Star Online* (May 19, 2011). [online] http://thestar.com.my/news/story.asp?file=/2011/5/19/nation/20110519095125&sec=nation. Accessed April 5, 2013.

Sayson, Ian. "Philippine Stocks to Overtake Economy This Year: Southeast Asia." *Bloomberg News* (March 7, 2013). [online] http://www.bloomberg.com/news/2013-03-06/philippine-stocks-to-overtake-economy-this-year-southeast-asia.html. Accessed June 2, 2013.

Setiawati, Indah. "General Motors Indonesia to Produce 40,000 Cars at Bekasi Plant." *Jakarta Post* (August 12, 2011). [online] http://www.thejakartapost.com/news/2011/08/12/general-motors-indonesia-produce-40000-cars-bekasi-plant.html. Accessed April 10, 2013.

"U.S. Apparel Imports from Vietnam Continue to Surge: Up 26%." *American Chamber of Commerce Vietnam* (2012). [online] http://www.amchamvietnam.com/1779. Accessed March 5, 2013.

"U.S. Relations with Malaysia." *U.S. Department of State* (October 24, 2012). [online] http://www.state.gov/r/pa/ei/bgn/2777.htm. Accessed June 2, 2013.

"Walmart China Factsheet." *Walmart* (n.d.). [online] http://www.wal-martchina.com/english/walmart/index.htm. Accessed April 4, 2013.

"Walmart U.S. Stores." *Walmart* (2012). [online] http://corporate.walmart.com/our-story/our-stores/united-states-stores. Accessed April 2, 2013.

Wang, Jin. "The Economic Impact of Special Economic Zones: Evidence from Chinese Municipalities." *London School of Economics* (November 2009).

"What Is the Value of International Students to Your State in 2012?" *NAFSA* (2013). [online] http://www.nafsa.org/Explore_International_Education/Impact/ Data_And_Statistics/What_Is_the_Value_ f_International_Students_to_Your_State_in_2012_. Accessed April 4, 2013.

Williams, Brock. "Trans-Pacific Partnership (TPP) Countries: Comparative Trade and Economic Analysis." *Congressional Research Service* (January 29, 2013). pp. 1–12.

CHAPTER 4

"Annual Report to Congress: Military and Security Developments Involving the People's Republic of China 2011." *Department of Defense* (May 6, 2012). [online] http:// www.defense.gov/pubs/pdfs/2011_CMPR_Final.pdf. Accessed November 5, 2012.

Armstrong, Benjamin. "China . . . from the Sea: The Importance of Chinese Naval History." *Strategic Insights*, vol. 6, no. 7 (December 2007). [online] http:// www.dtic.mil/cgi-bin/GetTRDoc?AD=ADA519989. Accessed April 12, 2013.

Bedford, Christian. "The View from the West: Chinese Naval Power in the 21st Century." *Canadian Naval Review*, vol. 5, no. 2 (Summer 2009). pp. 34–35. [online] http:// www.navalreview.ca/wp-content/uploads/public/vol5num2/vol5num2art8.pdf. Accessed April 9, 2012.

Central Intelligence Agency. "China." *World Factbook* (2013). [online] https:// www.cia.gov/library/publications/the world-factbook/geos/ch.html. Accessed March 31, 2013.

"China's Anti-Piracy Role off Somalia Expands." *BBC News* (January 29, 2010).

"Chinese Navy Sails Another First off Somalia." *Wall Street Journal* (March 30, 2011).

"A Country Study: China." *Library of Congress Country Studies* (August 24, 2012). [online] http://lcweb2.loc.gov/frd/cs/cntoc.html. Accessed March 24, 2013.

Daniels, Christopher L. *Somali Piracy and Terrorism in the Horn of Africa* (Lanham, MD: Scarecrow Press, 2012).

"The Dragon's New Teeth: A Rare Look inside the World's Biggest Military Expansion." *The Economist* (April 17, 2012). [online] http://www.economist.com/node/ 21552193. Accessed November 3, 2012.

Glass, Andrew. "House Approves Formosa Resolution, Jan. 25, 1955." *Politico* (January 25, 2011). [online] http://www.politico.com/news/stories/0111/48058.html. Accessed April 12, 2013.

Hartnett, Daniel M., and Frederic Vellucci. "Towards a Maritime Strategy: An Analysis of Chinese Views since the Early 1990's." In Phillip C. Saunders, Christopher D. Yung, Michael Swaine, and Andrew Nein-Dzu Yang, eds. *The Chinese Navy: Expanding Capabilities, Evolving Roles* (Washington, DC: National Defense University Press, 2011), pp. 81–82.

"Korean War." *History* (2013). [online] http://www.history.com/topics/korean-war. Accessed April 12, 2012.

Li, Nan. "The Evolution of China's Naval Strategy and Capabilities: From 'Near Coast' and 'Near Seas' to 'Far Seas.'" In Phillip C. Saunders, Christopher D. Yung, Michael Swaine, and Andrew Nein-Dzu Yang, eds. *The Chinese Navy: Expanding Capabilities, Evolving Roles* (Washington, DC: National Defense University Press, 2011), pp. 111–16.

"Milestones: 1953–1960." *U.S. Department of State, Office of the Historian* (n.d.). [online] http://history.state.gov/milestones/1953-1960/TaiwanSTraitCrises. Accessed April 12, 2013.

"Taiwan Strait: 21 July 1995 to 23 March 1996." *Global Security.org* (2013). [online] http:/ /www.globalsecurity.org/military/ops/taiwan_strait.htm. Accessed April 12, 2013.

Zageria, Donald S. *Breaking the China–Taiwan Impasse* (Westport, CT: Praeger, 2003).

CHAPTER 5

"The Bombing of Hiroshima and Nagasaki." *History* (2013). [online] http://www.history.com/topics/bombing-of-hiroshima-and-nagasaki. Accessed April 15, 2013.

Central Intelligence Agency. "Guam." *World Factbook* (2013). [online] https://www.cia.gov/library/publications/the-world factbook/geos/my.html. Accessed, March 29, 2013.

Francisco, Luzviminda. "The First Vietnam: U.S.–Philippine War of 1899." *History Is a Weapon* (1973). [online] http://historyisaweapon.com/defcon1/franciscofirstvietnam.html. Accessed April 10, 2013.

"Guadalcanal Campaign, August 1942–February 1943, Overview and Special Image Selection." *Naval History and Heritage Command* (n.d.). [online] http://www.history.navy.mil/photos/events/wwii-pac/guadlcnl/guadlcnl.htm. Accessed April 15, 2013.

"History." *Naval Base Guam* (n.d.). [online] http://www.cnic.navy.mil/Guam/AboutUs/History/index.htm. Accessed April 12, 2013.

"Japan: World War II and the Occupation, 1941–52." *Library of Congress Country Studies* (January 1994). [online] http://lcweb2.loc.gov/cgi-bin/query/r?frd/cstdy:@field(DOCID+jp0046). Accessed, March 24, 2013.

"Korean War." *History* (2013). [online] http://www.history.com/topics/korean-war. Accessed April 10, 2013.

"The Korean War, June 1950–July 1953." *Naval Heritage and History Command* (n.d.). [online] http://www.history.navy.mil/photos/events/kowar/kowar.htm. Accessed April 12, 2013.

Lotz, David, and Rose S. N. Manibusan. "Liberation—Guam Remembers." *National Park Service* (n.d.). [online] http://www.nps.gov/history/history/online_books/npswapa/extContent/Lib/liberation16.htm. Accessed April 15, 2013.

MacMillan, Margaret. *Nixon and Mao: The Week That Changed the World* (New York: Random House, 2007), pp. xvi–xxii.

"Milestones: 1945–1952." *U.S. Department of State, Office of the Historian* (n.d.). [online] http://history.state.gov/milestones/1945-1952/JapanReconstruction. Accessed April 15, 2013.

"The Obama Administration's Pivot to Asia." *The Foreign Policy Initiative* (2010). [online] http://www.foreignpolicyi.org/content/obama-administrations-pivot-asia. Accessed April 17, 2013.

"Pearl Harbor." *History* (2013). [online] http://www.history.com/topics/pearl-harbor. Accessed June 5, 2013.

"The Philippine–American War, 1899–1902." *U.S. Department of State, Office of the Historian* (n.d.). [online] http://history.state.gov/milestones/1899-1913/War. Accessed April 13, 2013.

"The Philippine War: A Conflict of Conscience for African Americans." *National Park Service* (2013). [online] http://www.nps.gov/prsf/historyculture/the-philippine-in-surrectiothe-philippine-war-a-conflict-of-consciencen-a-war-of-controversy.htm. Accessed April 13, 2013.

"Philippines: World War II, 1941–45." *Library of Congress Country Studies* (June 1991). [online] http://lcweb2.loc.gov/cgi-bin/query/r?frd/cstdy:@field(DOCID+ph0033). Accessed March 24, 2013.

San Juan, E., Jr. "U.S. Genocide in the Philippines: A Case of Guilt, Shame, or Amnesia?" *Selves and Others* (March 22, 2005). [online] http://web.archive.org/web/20080430182246/http://www.selvesandothers.org/article9315.html. Accessed April 5, 2013.

"South Korea: The Korean War, 1950–53." *Library of Congress Country Studies* (June 1990). [online] http://lcweb2.loc.gov/cgi-bin/query/r?frd/cstdy:@field(DOCID+kr0026). Accessed March 24, 2013.

"U.S. Army Campaigns: WWII—Asiatic-Pacific Theater." *U.S. Army Center of Military History* (November 19, 2010). [online] http://www.history.army.mil/html/reference/army_flag/ww2_ap.html. Accessed April 10, 2013.

"U.S., China Mark 30th Anniversary of Normalized Relations." *Voice of America* (October 27, 2009). [online] http://www.voanews.com/content/a-13-2008-12-15-voa39-66618542/556463.html. Accessed April 17, 2013.

"Vietnam War." *History* (2013). [online] http://www.history.com/topics/vietnam-war. Accessed April 10, 2013.

CHAPTER 6

Alessi, Christopher, and Stephanie Hanson. "Expanding China–Africa Oil Ties," *Council on Foreign Relations* (February 8, 2012). [online] http://www.cfr.org/china/expanding-china-africa-oil-ties/p9557. Accessed April 21, 2013.

Central Intelligence Agency. "China." *World Factbook* (2013). [online] https://www.cia.gov/library/publications/the-world-factbook/geos/ch.html. Accessed March 29, 2013.

———. "Indonesia." *World Factbook* (2013). [online] https://www.cia.gov/library/publications/the-world-factbook/geos/id.html. Accessed March 29, 2013.

———. "Vietnam." *World Factbook* (2013). [online] https://www.cia.gov/library/publications/the-world-factbook/geos/vm.html. Accessed March 29, 2013.

"China Begins to Lose Edge as World's Factory Floor." *Wall Street Journal* (January 16, 2013). [online] http://online.wsj.com/article/SB10001424127887323783704578245241751969774.html. Accessed April 19, 2013.

"A Country Study: China." *Library of Congress Country Studies* (August 24, 2012). [online] http://lcweb2.loc.gov/frd/cs/cntoc.html. Accessed March 24, 2013.

"Declaration on the Conduct of Parties in the South China Sea." *Association of Southeast Asian Nations* (2012). [online] http://www.asean.org/asean/external-relations/china/item/declaration-on-the-conduct-of-parties-in-the-south-china-sea. Accessed April 26, 2013.

Malanczuk, Peter. *Akehurst's Modern Introduction to International Law* (New York: Routledge, 1997).

Olesen, Alexa. "Shansha, China's New 'City,' Strengthens Country's Foothold in Disputed Waters." *The Huffington Post* (July 24, 2012). [online] http://www.huffingtonpost.com/2012/07/24/sansha-china_n_1697523.html. Accessed April 25, 2013.

Sentana, Made. "Indonesia Foreign Direct Investment Hits High." *Wall Street Journal* (January 22, 2013). [online] http://online.wsj.com/article/SB10001424127887324624404578257212289247592.html. Accessed April 19, 2013.

Severino, Rodolfo. "A Code of Conduct for the South China Sea." *Center for Strategic and International Studies, PacNet*, Number 45A (August 17, 2012).

Spegel, Brian. "New Tensions Rise on the South China Sea." *Wall Street Journal* (August 5, 2012). [online] http://online.wsj.com/article/SB10000872396390443659204577570514282930558.html. Accessed April 25, 2013.

Steinbock, Daniel. "Foreign Investment Relocates in China and Asia." *EconoMonitor* (February 27, 2013). [online] http://www.economonitor.com/blog/2013/02/foreign-investment-relocates-in-china-and-asia. Accessed April 19, 2013.

Thuy, Tran Truong. "Recent Developments in the South China Sea: Implications for Regional Security and Cooperation." *Center for Strategic and International Studies, Southeast Asia Program* (n.d.). [online] http://csis.org/files/publication/110629_Thuy_South_China_Sea.pdf. Accessed April 26, 2013.

Tofani, Robert. "Ambiguity Afloat in the South China Sea," *Asia Times* (April 24, 2013). [online] http://www.atimes.com/atimes/Southeast_Asia/SEA-01-240413.html. Accessed April 25, 2013.

Yap, Karl Lester M. "Abe's Japanese Stimulus Seen Boosting Southeast Asia." *Bloomberg News* (January 21, 2013). [online] http://www.bloomberg.com/news/2013-01-20/ japan-s-stimulus-seen-boosting-southeast-asia-as-korea-suffers.html. Accessed April 21, 2013.

Index

About the Author

Dr. Christopher L. Daniels is professor of political science in the Center for Global Security and International Affairs at Florida A&M University. He received his doctorate from Howard University and has traveled to; conducted research on; and given lectures about security, governance, and economic development in several countries across the world. He also has given lectures at several American universities and conducted training programs for government employees. He began his professorial career at Georgetown University in the School of Foreign Service, and in April 2012 he published his first book, *Somali Piracy and Terrorism in the Horn of Africa* (Scarecrow Press).